Love

A Reason to Live

Samuel C Cowgill

Published by Litnum Publications
22 Hillcrest Avenue, Scarborough
North Yorkshire YO12 6RQ

www.litnumpublications.co.uk

British Library Cataloguing in Publication Data
A catalogue record for this book is available from the British Library.

ISBN 978-09557664-7-3

Cover design and type set by S C Cowgill
Printed in Great Britain by
Berforts Information Press Ltd
www.berforts.com

Acknowledgements

It's my privilege to sincerely thank:

Ivan and Daphne for entrusting me to write your incredible story,

Solomon and Sweta for your inside story from the orphanage which continues to move and inspire,

Angelo for introducing me to Ivan and Daphne,

Margaret for your proofreading,

readers for buying the book,

Jesus for allowing me to record these biographies and for your faithfulness throughout the time of writing.

I cannot conclude without thanking my wife, Veronica for her unswerving support. Spending long, lonely hours while I wrote is a tremendous sacrifice.

Samuel C Cowgill
November 2014

Dedicated to the children and widows of the
Spirit of Liberty Children's Home

Proceeds to the Spirit of Liberty Children's Home

Contents

Refugees

Darkness prevailed but not night, as the winter sun beamed across the small, Italian coastal town of Formia. Nature's elements were not to blame for the despair that gripped the populous. Hearts beat heavily and stomachs churned incessantly as the news of enforced evacuation spread contagiously.

The streets heaved with people struggling with what they could carry to board the array of locally commandeered trucks.

'Schnell! Schnell!'

Rifle butts enforced words as soldiers jostled the crowd. Swastikas flew high as foreign troops drove frightened residents from their homes. Amidst alarm and confusion, a woman carrying a large bundle, fearfully gathered her six children around her - the eldest equally as bewildered as the youngest about their fate.

'You must board the wagon,' urged the driver as frightened neighbours clambered aboard.

'I'll not leave without Enrico!' said the woman.

'Crazy woman!' he snapped, gesticulating his annoyance.

'Einsteigen!' demanded a soldier brandishing his rifle as an impetus to get people aboard.

'Lass sie hinter sich!' demanded his commander, insisting that they be left behind. Turning to the woman, he said in fluent Italian, 'We can't wait. If he's not here shortly, you and your family must board the wagon.'

'I'll do no such thing!' she screamed hysterically. 'I'll not leave without him.'

'You stubborn woman!' screeched a neighbour as she clambered onto the wagon. 'Do you want to die?'

In defiance, the woman stood firm.

'I'll go and get him, Ma,' said Rina, her eldest teenage daughter.

'No! We must stay together. Your papa won't be long.'

'I'll go see where he is, Mrs Squillino,' volunteered a youth.

'Two minutes! That's all you've got,' said the officer.

'He's at the shop collecting his scissors and things,' shouted Mrs Squillino as the lad sped up the cobbled incline. His stride sure, his face aptly projected the urgency of his task. Breathless on reaching the barber's shop, he entered.

'Mr Squillino, the wagons are leaving. Your wife and children are waiting for you. She refuses to leave without you. You must come now before it's too late.'

Grabbing his hairdressing implements, he glanced around the shop, hoping it would be there on his return. Locking the door, he rushed to join his family. 'I'm sorry, Antonietta,' he said apologetically, giving her a reassuring hug. 'Did we lock the house door?'

'We did. They wanted us to board the trucks, but I refused to leave without you!'

Smiling, he lifted the little ones of his brood onto the wagon. Rina and Tommaso, older than Gino and Sergio, were of an age to understand the severity of the situation. Five-year-old Enzo and his younger sister Laura, however, would hold only scant recollections of that dreadful day.

To those around her, Antonietta projected confidence. Hiding her distress, she had bravely stood her ground when confronted by the military. Fear of what would

8

become of her family bubbled relentlessly below the surface. Antonietta had a secret.

Ensuring his children were safely aboard the wagon, Enrico smiled, with his eyes on Antonietta.

I love you too, was her silent reply.

Deeply in love with his one and only sweetheart, a glorious smile was reciprocated.

'I know.' Touching her cheek tenderly, his dark brown eyes were ablaze with overflowing affection.

'Don't worry. We'll be fine. Believe me.'

His flock safely aboard, Enrico settled Antonietta comfortably on their bundles of clothes before climbing aboard himself. The lifting of the tailboard and the turning of the engine accompanied by a plume of exhaust fumes heralded the beginning of a long and arduous journey to an unknown destination.

Reaching the outskirts of town, Antonietta asked, 'Where are they taking us, Enrico?'

'I don't know. Somewhere north, I think.'

A grievous time had beset them. Many hardships and uncertainty would prevail before peace would break the curse of conflict. War had come. The invasion of Italy had begun.

The Futility of War

Built on the peninsula jutting into the Mediterranean north of Naples and only 5.95 kilometres north of Formia, the historical town of Gaeta had been a stronghold of Mussolini until the new, fragile government had imprisoned him on the island of Ponza. The Italians had ceased fighting, but the war on mainland Italy was about to begin. Taking advantage of their superior strength, those who had fought beside them had become their enemy.

To defend the backdoor to the Fatherland, the occupying army drew up three lines of defence. The most formidable, the Gustav Line, ran across the narrowest point of Italy along the Garigliano River from the Tyrrhenian Sea in the west, through the Apennine Mountains anchoring on Monte Casino and eastward to the mouth of the Sangro River on the Adriatic coast.

Recognising its strategic importance and fearful of an allied landing in that area, German troops occupying Gaeta had expelled most of the population. The zone of exclusion that began with a five-kilometre border from the historic city centre soon stretched to Formia. The Nazi commanders had ordered the remaining citizens to leave the area. Those who would not comply were forcefully removed to concentration camps. Some were sent to Germany.

War had raged in Europe for almost four years. The German and Italian campaign in North Africa had failed and the might of other nations now threatened them. Allied troops in control of Sicily had their eye on Rome. The Italian fascist dictator imprisoned, the new government argued indecisively and made tragic mistakes.

When the fledgling government of Italy declared war on Nazi Germany, the German command sprung the fascist dictator from prison. With much gusto, Mussolini set up a republic in northern Italy and fought alongside the enemy.

The Squillino family had known little of the dictates of a fascist regime. They were ordinary people struggling to nurture and feed their family in an honest and loving way. Politics and power was not what they craved. Like so many, they had shied away from comment or support of authoritarian fascists' aspirations.

The long haul north towards the mountains of Tuscany took its toll. Darkness had fallen over the hilltop town of Montepulciano when the wagons pulled into the square. Tired and hungry, the occupants fixed their thoughts on where they would sleep and where their next meal would come from. Some were fortunate to have relatives in the town, but not the Squillino family. Refugees in their own country, they were destitute and in desperate need of someone to love them. An unspoken question lingered in Enrico and Antonietta's thoughts, *Who would or could welcome two adults and six children into their home?*

As the wagons drew up in front of the Gothic portal of the 13th century convent of St. Agnes, a number of inquisitive nuns ran out to investigate the disturbance. A flurry of activity followed as the human cargo was gradually shed before leaving to pick up more evacuees.

'Out!' yelled the driver.

The square was almost empty when Enrico helped his exhausted Antonietta before waking those of his children who were asleep. With hope that someone had arranged accommodation for his family, he motioned to the driver.

'Where do we go?'

'Don't ask me! I'm finished here.'

At that, he jumped into his vehicle and drove off, leaving the eight alone and destitute.

Seeing their plight, and overwhelmed with compassion, a young nun beckoned the others of the convent. 'Quickly! Quickly! You see to the children! I'll help the man and his wife.'

Tenderly, the nuns escorted their unsolicited deliveries into the convent. Some carried the bleary-eyed children across the cobbles while others carried the family's possessions. Once inside the stone building, a plethora of activity erupted as more nuns and novices scurried around attending to their guests.

'What's all this noise?' snapped Mother Superior.

Everyone stood still. With stomachs churning, all fell quiet.

A compassionate nun broke the silence.

'This woman needs our help. We could not leave her or her family out in the square. How could we say, 'There is no room at the inn,' when we have food and shelter? Surely it cannot be right?'

Tense moments prevailed. Mother Superior's face set. The nervous atmosphere hardened as silence again fell.

'We'll leave,' said Enrico. 'We don't want to be a burden to you or cause trouble.'

Gathering his brood, he headed for the door. The strained silence lengthened. Tears filled the kind-hearted. Many questioned, *Is love and compassion dead?*

'Stop! I was wrong. You can stay.'

Enrico saw that a big smile adorned her face.

'Come along! We have much to do to make our guests welcome.'

The strained moments confined to history, everyone breathed easily.

'You three go and organise food for these little ones. You four sort out the sleeping arrangements. The rest of you are to make our guests welcome by doing whatever is necessary. Well! Don't just stand there. Jump to it!'

Enrico was relieved that the compassionate act of strangers had saved the family from enforced separation.

As the months drifted by, they settled well in their new surroundings. The sound of children's feet running around the ancient convent echoed a sweet song amidst the ravages of war. Food was always scarce. When particularly hard to come by, Enrico would forfeit his share for Antonietta and his children.

'You're looking shabby, Enrico.'

Antonietta was used to seeing him clean-shaven. She'd rarely seen him bearded - hardly an advertisement for a barber!

'You need a shave. Then I'll see much more of you.'

His eyes lit up with a beaming smile.

Nothing more was said. Enrico continued to grow his beard beyond mid-chest length, making him look much older than his thirty-eight years. Jobless and without the means of making a living, a few older men let him cut their hair. Sometimes he would sit with the locals around the square, chatting. One day, while in conversation with a few of his acquaintances, the sound of army trucks seized his attention.

'They're coming!' blurted out a local, dashing home.

Before Enrico could rush away, two heavy army trucks had entered the square, fronted by an armoured vehicle flying the swastika. He sat tightly on his seat, hoping not to draw attention to himself. He thought better of wanting to hide behind the ornate well nearby.

A number of soldiers wielding rifles jumped from the trucks. Bursting into the houses and dragging out screaming men, women and children, they forced them to board.

Enrico's heart pounded heavily when two soldiers approached him. The roundup of the old and young continued, their horrific cries echoing around the square.

One of the soldiers gestured aggressively to Enrico to see his papers. Enrico shrugged his shoulders as if not to understand. The soldier moved to strike him. Suddenly, Enrico clutched his chest. His face contorted as if in great pain, he dropped to the ground as if dead.

From across the square the officer beckoned to leave him. Soon the soldiers were gone, allowing the tranquil atmosphere to return.

Seeing Enrico prostrate on the cobbles, a number of concerned friends ran to tend him.

'He's dead,' said the first.

Double Joy

'We need to get him off these cobbles.'

Concerned friends stooped to lift Enrico. Suddenly, he gasped for breath. He opened his eyes. A huge grin lit up his face.

'I'm fine,' he said to his astonished friends. 'Thanks for your help and concern.'

Relieved that he was alive, everyone laughed when realising what he had done.

'When those soldiers came, I trembled so much I didn't know where to run. When that fellow set his fist to hit me, down I went, not daring to move a muscle until they had gone. I'm sorry if I scared you. They terrified me.'

'I saw you drop. I thought you were dead. Are you sure you are all right?'

'I'm fine. Truly! I'm fine.'

Enrico rushed to tell Antonietta of his ordeal before some other frightened her into thinking he had suffered some serious affliction. Feigning death a second time would be much harder than the first. His acting alone had not saved him. A combination of dramatics and split second timing when the officer shouted to leave him may well have helped. Perhaps his unkempt beard had played its part in keeping him safe.

Enrico relaxed despite knowing they would return. They did. On several occasions they sought out members of the resistance, civilians and Jews.

All were suspect. The concentration camp at Fossil in northern Italy had plenty of room for dissenters. The regime had extended the camp to accommodate an influx of Italians, Jews and political opponents of the

Nazi regime - mostly en route to the extermination camps in Germany and Poland.

The area around Montepulciano was active with the resistant movement, especially to the west where numerous skirmishes with the fascists occurred. It was a perilous time for the Squillino family.

Enrico had noticed Antonietta's pale complexion beneath her swarthy skin, but said nothing. He'd seen the signs before. It was not until her early morning sickness started that Antonietta confessed to the cause. Fearful of what his reaction would be, she'd struggled on, not knowing how to tell him.

Normally he would welcome the news. When alone with him, she said boldly, 'I'm carrying our child.'

Antonietta was unaware of his thoughts as Enrico stood gazing at her, not blinking an eye. Taking her in his arms he stroked her face and said lovingly, 'Wonderful! Now we have another reason to live.' For a few brief moments, their dire circumstances dissipated as they held one another in sweet embrace. 'We'll have to tell the children,' he smiled. 'When is he due?'

'Sometime mid-September. What makes you say it's a boy?'

'I have a feeling. He'll be here in six months.'

Holding her in his arms, and gently caressing her face, he asked, 'What's wrong?'

'You know me well.'

'I hope so. You are my wife and my love.'

'I was thinking of Antonio and how I loved him. He was such a lovely child.'

Enrico took her in his arms again.

'Please, don't be sad. We must not question why he died.'

She raised a smile at his reassurance.

'You're having a baby! A new life, Antonietta - a life longing to be loved and nurtured. We've work to do. We must be ready for my last son,' assured Enrico - more as self-affirmation.

Enrico didn't care what the nuns thought. The pending arrival of his eighth child spurred him on to find some way to lift his family out of their poverty. War or no war, he was determined to secure each child's future in an uncertain world.

Antonietta was as determined as Enrico to make sure her children would not be a burden to anyone. She worked hard throughout her pregnancy and thanked God that He had protected them from harm. Despite her busy workload, she always found time to pray. Even in her darkest moments, she never forgot to speak to her Maker. He was her strength, more than Enrico. She depended on Him to keep the family safe and well.

All the Squillino children had been born in Formia. Antonietta wanted her eighth child to be born there too, but that was not possible due to prevailing war.

Relatively safe, high on the mountain ridge at Montepulciano, only hope remained.

The guns of war were fast approaching. News of the bombing of the 13th century monastery at Monte Casino and the death of many children there did nothing to ease their plight. They too might have died, had the Nazis taken them there.

Bitter battles fought at Anzio and the obliteration of Monte Casino brought no peace to the ill-fated people of Italy, as foreign armies moved north. Nothing was sacred. After the fall of Rome, the Nazis formed a new line of defence. The Trasimene Line north of Rome ran south of Ancona on the east coast, westward past the southern shores of Lake Trasimeno near Perugia and on towards the west coast south of Grosseto.

Montepulciano lay just above the Trasimene Line as the liberating forces advanced northward.

The war lingered on and at times there were periods of inactivity. It was a time of win a little, lose a little, win it back and lose it again. Food, clothing and shelter became scarce as news of fighting brought the fear of street warfare nearer to Montepulciano.

There were fierce battles in the valleys of Tuscany. News that the Trasimene Line was broken brought some relief. The war for the Squillino family was at an end, but not for those living further north as the Nazi regime set up a third defence - the Gothic Line.

Labour of Love

As the summer months faded and the autumn equinox approached, a fresh breath of hope filled the convent. In the early hours of Sunday morning Antonietta woke to discover her waters had broken.

There was much scurrying around as the nuns rushed to prepare for the delivery, while others gossiped the news throughout the convent. A buzz of excitement filled the air and a sense of joy blossomed at the thought of the birth of a new life.

'Ooh! That hurt,' winced Antonietta trying to be brave as the painful contractions grew stronger.

'You'll not be wanted for some time,' said a nun to Enrico as she and a novice walked Antonietta along a corridor to a small room lit by the sun gleaming through an elongated stained glass window.

Safely on the bed, Antonietta rested, holding her tummy. 'Oh! There's another.'

'You should be used to the pain by now,' said a well-rounded nun more akin to a sumo wrestler.

'I'll take over now,' she said, motioning to the other to leave.

'Bring a bowl and towels,' she ordered with the authority and knowledge of a professional midwife. 'You'll be fine,' she said, fussing around the bed.

'It will arrive when ready. Boy or girl, they're all the same when they get here. A burden to the arms and a worry for the soul. Put them there,' she pointed to the table on seeing the novice return with a bowl and towels. 'Have you seen a birth before?'

'Three. All my sisters.'

'Then you can stay and help.'

The young novice took hold of Antonietta's hand and gave her a reassuring smile.

'I'll cut your nails. It will help take your mind off the pain.'

'Nonsense!' snapped the nun.

Giving a friendly shrug, the novice made no response. 'My mum almost cut my hand with her nails when my youngest sister arrived. She gripped me so tightly I thought my hand would drop off.'

Antonietta smiled knowingly. Her nails cut, pain followed. 'My contractions are getting stronger.'

'Good! We'll not have long to wait.'

Four hours passed and still no sign of the baby. Mother Superior popped her head around the door. 'Nothing yet, I assume?'

'Not yet,' replied the nun.

'I have an anxious father out here, pacing the corridors.'

'Tell him I'm doing fine,' smiled Antonietta. 'Tell him I love him.'

'I guess it'll be a boy,' announced the seemingly knowledgeable nun.

'My husband says it's a boy. What makes *you* think my baby is a boy?' asked Antonietta, as the pain intensified.

'Boys are lazy on arrival and throughout life.'

'It could be a girl,' said Antonietta between deep breaths to offset the pain. 'You don't like boys?'

'They have their place - not that I would know much about males. My father was a drunk and my mother a saintly person. A perfect match, would you not say? My perception of men is somewhat tainted.'

'Ouch! I think it's time.'

'Push, girl! Push!' screamed the nun. 'It's on its way. I can see its head. Push, girl! Push!'

With one final deep breath and strenuous expulsion, the baby arrived.

'It's a boy! It's a boy! What time is it?'

'Nine o'clock,' came the reply.

The umbilical cord tied and cut, a far greater attachment followed as baby and mother became entwined in love.

'What will you call him?' asked the novice.

Cradling her baby in her arms with the pain of childbearing fading, Antonietta gently stroked his cheek. She admired his dark brown eyes and delicate facial features. Content, she was thankful he was as God had intended - perfectly formed in His image.

'His name is Ivan,' she announced. Her joy transmitted passionately through her words. 'Ivan Squillino. Yes! Ivan Squillino is his name.'

Ivan thrived. There were plenty of loving arms to share the workload of a new baby. Rina was an asset to her mother. The work did not stop her, however, from eyeing the local talent! Soon a number of boys took an interest in her. A handsome Tuscany lad stole her heart. Tommaso, the eldest son, did his share in caring for Ivan, as did Gino the eight-year old. Sergio, Enzo and Laura also played their part in loving the new arrival.

By the close of autumn, mother and baby were thriving. Certainly, Ivan had put on weight and made his presence known when demanding his feed.

Early one morning, Enrico sensed his wife was agitated.

'What's wrong?'

'I must go to church and thank God for Ivan's safe delivery. I'll be back before he wakes.'

Although it was 5.30 a.m., Enrico knew it was useless trying to stop her. He pulled the covers over his head and rolled over.

There were many astonished faces as Antonietta joined the nuns in the little sanctuary. From that day, she rose early to praise God for her family before returning to her room to prepare breakfast. There was always someone ready to speak of Antonietta's overwhelming capacity for motherhood.

The family was thankful for the food and a roof over their heads, despite the cramped accommodation. No one complained.

Hardship and Struggle

Following the Allied advance north across the Garigliano and then entering Rome, Enrico and Antonietta were overjoyed when told they were free to return home. The gossip on the tongues of those who had endured the enforced evacuation from their beloved Formia was rife.

The evacuees were thankful to the locals of Montepulciano for providing a welcome haven in their hour of need, but it was not home. Keen to return with the family, Enrico would happily have carried them through the passes and over the mountains on his shoulders, had it been possible.

Rumours of Allied troop movement and devastation in Gaeta and Formia circulated the hilltop retreat to the extent that Enrico decided to see for himself rather than drag the family away from the safety and stability of the convent.

'I'll return for you all when settled.'

There was little time for sentimentality when the families gathered in the Montepulciano square to wave their loved ones off. Devoid of carnival atmosphere, bunting or brass band, forced smiles masked the families' apprehension as an open-top wagon that was to take the men home appeared.

'I have to go now,' smiled Enrico, hugging Antonietta carefully so as not to squash the baby. A kiss on the cheek would have to suffice.

Longing to hug him, a slight crack in her voice betrayed her feelings.

'I love you.'

'I'll miss you,' he said as he lovingly wiped the teardrops from her cheek.

The pain of leaving the family was too much for Enrico when kissing each child. A momentary glance at Antonietta, he jumped onto the wagon that was to carry him south to Gaeta and then on to Formia.

Hiding his sorrow at leaving his family, he gave a reassuring wave as the wagon, fully loaded with returning companions, made its way out of the square.

As they chugged south, Enrico tried to picture in what state the town he loved would be in, and more so, his house.

The slow drive along winding roads on the back of an aging wagon was tiresome for its passengers, but the expectancy of reaching home kept their spirits high. Passing numerous convoys of motorised army personnel heading north was a fearful reminder that the war had not ended.

Anxiety heightened as they approached the outskirts of Gaeta. The picturesque landscape, the grassland, the trees, the cobbled streets and pan tiled roofed houses he had known so well were gone. Everywhere rang with a hollowness from the depressing greys.

Entering the town centre, rubble heaped upon rubble was all around him to the point that he lost his bearings. Cordite heavy in the air, burnt out military vehicles, bombed streets and flattened houses were all he could see as the wagon screeched to a halt.

'This is as far as I go,' announced the driver, dropping the tailgate.

'I thought you were going to Formia,' protested Enrico, supported by others.

'My orders were to bring you to Gaeta. Off you get. If you want to go to Formia, you'll have to walk.'

Unable to persuade the driver otherwise, disgruntled travellers jumped from the wagon. On terra firma, Enrico caught his bearings and headed south along the coastal road with others from his hometown.

On approaching Formia, Enrico could see that the place had fared no better in the conflict than Gaeta. Burnt out streets and bombed buildings were the norm. House upon house was nothing more than heaps of rubble - the occasional skeletal frame standing more akin to a medieval castle ruin. Even the bus terminal was in ruins, along with numerous burnt out buses. The unfamiliar twang of American talk filled the air where the military forces mustered.

Searching for where he thought his house and shop had stood, his eyes fixed on the rubble. He had been strong for his family for so long. Alone, empty and broken, he sank to his knees in despair, sobbing bitterly.

In desperation, he was determined not to let despondency weigh him down. Antonietta and his children were enough reason to grasp the few remaining threads of self-determination floating amidst his deep sense of hopelessness. Throwing off his depressive thoughts, he stood to his feet, resolved to face the future with vitality and vigour. With no place to rest for the night, he wandered aimlessly through the rubble.

By chance or by divine direction, Enrico met a cousin who offered him a small flat and a job in the physics section of the local education department. He seized both opportunities of accommodation and employment.

Working hard, he sent money to his family and visited whenever possible.

Weeks slipped into months, and then a ray of normality shone through. Rina announced she was to marry. Enrico and Antonietta had no reason to refuse the union and the pair was married in Montepulciano. Their wedding was a joyous occasion.

Enrico was in Montepulciano when Antonietta spotted a football coupon protruding from his pocket. Saying nothing, she decided to confront him when least expected. He was drying the dishes when she pounced.

'I see you're doing those silly football coupons. You'll never win. You might as well throw your money down the drain.'

'I have to try something for a little extra cash. All I need is 13 points to win the jackpot.'

'You'll be fortunate to get two points with your luck.'

Enrico shrugged his shoulders. 'It's worth a try.'

'More like a waste of time.'

'Would you prefer I stop trying?'

'Do what you want to, if it makes you happy.' Nothing more was said.

Two challenging years passed buy. Throughout Enrico's absence, Antonietta continued to rise early with the nuns to pray for her family. She thanked God when Enrico wrote to say he had rented a larger property in the village of Scauri.

Robbed of their life in Formia, it was now time to start anew. Within weeks, Antonietta and the children journeyed to an unknown future. Ivan was three years old.

The re-uniting was a joyous occasion. Adjusting to new surroundings, the family started to re-build the life they had enjoyed before their enforced evacuation.

The house was barely big enough for everyone, but larger than their accommodation at the convent. Antonietta was grateful to have Enrico at her side. Faithful to her promise, she rose early each morning to pray at the local church before returning home to prepare the breakfast, clean the house, do the washing, make the meals and generally see to the family's needs. Even when desperate for cash, she never let her children know of the difficulties. The children lacked for nothing they needed. Anything they desired had to wait until spare funds were available. Even in difficult times, Antonietta always ensured her children were well dressed. It was a time to build new relationships, make new friends and thank God for keeping them safe through a war.

With eight mouths to feed and food in short supply, meal times were a constant worry. Tommaso helped by slipping out to a nearby farm and returning with a few tomatoes, vegetables and a little fruit. Assuming that everything was kosher, no questions were asked about how he'd paid for them. Antonietta was grateful for whatever she could get to feed the family.

Such was her love for her children, whenever one or the other was sick or had toothache she would pray that the illness and pain they suffered would transfer to her. She believed in the power of prayer and had many answers to her petitioning. The anchor of the family, she went about the daily duties of caring for her children and creating a happy, stable environment in which they could thrive.

By the time Ivan started school, stability had returned to the family. Everyone was delighted when Enrico brought home a small radio. Well-used, it was an asset for listening to the national news and fun for the young ones with their music.

Pain and Joy

The years Ivan had spent in the convent were locked deep in his memory. By the age of eight he was showing signs of growing into a strong, slimly built handsome young child. Loving the clean outdoor environment, he readily confessed to not being one for hard study. Besides his physical progress, he had developed a youthful, playful defiance that invariably invited trouble - certainly the teaching nuns thought so!

The comings and goings of the older children made it almost an impossible task for the family to gather collectively at mealtimes. To maintain some regularity, Enrico set a family rule. Without exception, each Sunday, family members were to be sat at the lunch table by 1 p.m. The arrangement worked well.

One Sunday, while everyone was enjoying their meal, Enrico suddenly dropped his knife and fork. Clutching his chest, he let out a huge sigh.

Antonietta sprang to her feet. 'What's wrong?' Concerned faces reflected their mother's anxiety.

Unable to speak, he continued to grasp his chest. Anxious moments lengthened. The pain easing, he picked up his cutlery.

'There. The pain has gone. It's nothing. Just a bit of heartburn.'

Antonietta was not convinced.

'You're working too hard, Enrico. You need to rest. I insist you visit the doctor and let him check you out.'

'You've room to talk. You've never been to a doctor in your life. I tell you. It's just a touch of heartburn.'

A few weeks later, she was troubled. Although she never complained, Enrico always knew when she was worried about things.

'What's wrong, Antonietta? Have I said something to hurt you?'

She ventured a smile. 'No. I'm worried about the money and food situation. I'm at my wits end wondering how to feed the children when what little we have has gone. The children are growing out of their clothes. Even the *hand me downs* are in short supply.'

'Try not to worry. We've had less before and survived. Something will turn up. You'll see. If things come to the worst, I can go without, as you do.'

'I don't.'

'Yes you do. I've seen how you slip a little more onto the children's plates and then go without yourself.'

'That's what mothers do.'

Enrico took her in his arms. The problem was not resolved, but Antonietta felt much better after sharing her worries.

The following Saturday evening Enrico listened to the football results. As the announcer said each score, he marked off his coupon, demanding hush from the children until he had finished checking the scores. Tense and excited, he had nine points.

'Come on! Four more points will do,' he encouraged the wireless commentator.

'Yes!' he shouted, breaking his own rule of silence as the announcer added another point to his score of nine. 'Three more! That's all I need!' There were only a few more scores to announce. Another point was added to his ten.

'Come on! Two more. Don't let me down.'

The points never came. Two short of the jackpot, the announcer ended his report.

Enrico was distraught. He had been so near, yet so far from being in the money. Convinced he would never again get so close to winning the jackpot, he checked and rechecked his coupon. There was no mistake - 11 points it was.

When rechecking for a third time, according to his reckoning, no punter had 13 points. Again, he rechecked his coupon and calculated that 11 points was the maximum any one could have. Doubt set in as he wondered if he was wrong. Saying nothing to Antonietta, he spent a nail-biting Sunday. By Monday evening, he had fallen out with doing the pools.

'You are right, Antonietta,' he said when eating his evening meal.

'Right about what?'

'The pools. It's a waste of time. I must be mad sitting here every Saturday marking off my coupon, hoping to win. I'll not do them again.'

Antonietta raised a smile as if to say, *I told you so*.

Early the following morning as Enrico prepared to go to work, there was a knock on his door.

'Is Mr Enrico Squillino in?' asked a smartly dressed man carrying a briefcase tucked under his arm.

Enrico thought it was some official from the local government. 'I am Mr Squillino.'

'Mr Enrico Squillino?'

'That's me.'

'May I come in?'

The man's voice demanded his attention. Without checking his credentials, Enrico showed him into the front room.

Fumbling in his briefcase, he pulled out an official document to which was attached a small slip of paper. By now, Antonietta had joined them.

'I need you to sign this,' said the man.

'What is it?'

'It's a receipt. I am from the football company. You've won 500 000 lira.'

Enrico could not believe his ears.

'Five hundred thousand lira!'

'That's right. I have the cheque here. As there was no outright winner on Saturday, and no one with 13 or 12 points, you share the jackpot with those who have eleven.'

'Sign the papers,' encouraged Antonietta, 'and let the man go.'

'A pen, a pen! I need a pen!'

The man handed Enrico his pen and watched as shaking hands scribbled on the dotted line. Enrico was about to hand the paper back when Antonietta snatched it from him.

'May I have the paper, Madam?'

'Not until you've handed him the cheque.'

'Of course! I almost forgot,' smiled the man jokingly.

With the cheque safely in Enrico's hand, Antonietta handed the man the paper. There would be no more scrimping and scraping to make ends meet - at least not for a little while!

A celebration was in order and much to talk about when Enrico returned from work. He'd spent a happy day thinking of all the things he could buy with his winnings - so had Antonietta! One of those new-fangled washing machines would help reduce the workload, and a fridge would offset the little waste they had. New clothes for her children were priorities - perhaps a new dress for herself and a coat for Enrico wouldn't go amiss.

The children were overjoyed at the news. Needs met and a few wants obtained, Enrico and Antonietta were careful as to how they spent the surplus.

Waywardness

Enrico had built many new relationships in his new surroundings. He loved the camaraderie, but never neglected his love for Antonietta or his children. He was surprised when he was contacted by one who asked to speak with him and Antonietta.

'Come in,' said Enrico, wondering why the man had called. 'This is my friend Fabrizzio,' he smiled, offering him a chair.

'Pleased to meet you,' said Antonietta. 'Would you like a coffee?'

'No thanks. I can't stay long.'

Antonietta sat beside Enrico, baffled as to why he had called.

'I have to go away on business for a few years and wondered if you would move into my villa.'

'Me! Rent your place?' Enrico shook his head. 'We'd love to, but cannot afford to rent such a large house?'

'No! No! No! It's not to rent. I need you to look after it while I'm away - as a sort of custodian - rent free.'

Enrico was more than interested. The villa was large enough for the children to have their own rooms. Attached was a furnished flat with a cellar.

'What do you think we should do, Antonietta?'

Her eyes beamed out the longings of her heart.

'The children would love the space.'

'We'll take your offer! Thank you for thinking of us.'

'Then I'll be off. We'll make the arrangements later.'

When Fabrizzio had gone, the pair could not believe their fortune. The children couldn't wait to move in.

The villa was all they wanted. Two houses joined by an internal door afforded plenty of space. The family was unrestricted.   There were also two holiday apartments.

Ivan had the full run of the place. He enjoyed using Gino's body building equipment in the cellar and was in the gym when two friends knocked on the door.
'Giovanni and Franco are here, Ma. Can I go out to play?'
  'It's Sunday.'
  'But Ma. I won't be long.'
  Ivan's persuasive tongue and bright eyes were enough to weaken his mother.
  'All right. Don't be late for lunch.'
  'I won't. I promise.'
  Off he ran with his friends to play amongst the rocks on the beach.
  The morning passed without incident and all was well. Sunday lunch was minutes away.
  'Where's Ivan?' asked Enrico as the rest of his children sat around the table ready to enjoy their meal. They waited as long as they could. Enrico was not happy. The meal was getting cold so they started without him.
  'I wonder where he's got to?' asked Laura.
  'He'll have forgotten the time,' said Antonietta, trying to lower the tension.
  By 3 p.m., Antonietta was becoming anxious.
  'What if something has happened to him?'
  'If anything had happened to him, we would know by now. He'll get a touch of my belt when he gets home.'
  'You're too harsh, Enrico. I'm worried.'
  'I'll go and look for him.'

Laura glanced out of the window and burst out laughing.

'What's wrong?' asked her mother.

'He's coming up the drive, drenched to the skin.'

The three rushed to the door.

'Where've you been?' screeched Enrico, dragging him into the house.

'I was playing amongst the rocks by the sea when I fell into the water.'

'Up those stairs. It's the strap for you and then bed.'

'I haven't had my lunch.'

'No! You're not having any. Up those stairs this minute and get dry!' shouted his papa.

Ivan darted to his bedroom in a flood of tears. The punishment was swift and on target. More tears streamed down his face. As soon as his papa had gone, Ivan slipped between the sheets, holding his backside to ease the pain.

Some time later, his papa entered the bedroom and sat on the bed. Ivan peeped over the covers.

'Do you know why I hit you, Ivan?'

'I fell in the water and got wet.'

'No.'

'It wasn't my fault. Giovanni pushed me.'

'Blaming others is not the thing to do. It's an excuse to hide behind to make you feel better. Your punishment is the result of disobedience. One hour a week to sit together as a family is all I ask, and you couldn't be bothered to honour my wishes.'

'But....'

'But nothing, Ivan. You're not telling me you played for two hours after falling into the water. You were drenched when you came home. The sun would have at least dried your hair. No, my lad. You rushed home the minute you got wet.'

Ivan had no defence. He knew his papa was right.

'What am I to do with you, Ivan?' he said with compassion in his voice. He leaned forward and stroked Ivan's cheek. 'You must learn to take responsibility for your actions. It's a lesson we all must learn. Your punishment is the consequence of your disobedience.'

'I'm sorry.'

'Saying sorry is not enough. You have to mean what you say.'

'I do, Papa.'

'Do you think I enjoy taking my belt to you? It breaks my heart, but you have to learn. Life is hard enough without courting trouble. I punished you because I love you.'

'What about the innocent who are punished?'

'What the innocent receive is not punishment but injustice. I love you, and always will. Rest now.'

Ivan considered every word his papa had said and held them in his heart. He tried to sleep, but hunger and thirst kept him awake.

Not long after, his mother entered carrying a tray.

'Sit up, Ivan. I've your dinner here for you.'

'Does papa know you're here?'

'Of course he does. He told me to keep it warm for you. He loves you as I do.'

Deception

Continuing to grow in strength and stature, Ivan had little appetite for serious study. A free spirit, he loved life and all it brought.

He was at school when an official-looking envelope dropped through the letterbox. Curious to read the contents, Antonietta ripped open the outer cover. Her heart sank when seeing the heading.

Department of Education

Dear Mr and Mrs Squillino,

On checking our records of your son Ivan's attendance, we note that he has been absent from school on several occasions without the customary explanatory letter.

Further to this, I have to inform you that on a number of occasions, he has been seen playing on the beach with friends during lesson time.

I remind you, absences from school are for illness and prearranged holiday periods; the latter being with my agreement.

I would be obliged if you would enlighten me as to the reason for your son's absences. I would appreciate an early reply.

Sincerely

Mr Russo. Head Teacher

Antonietta shivered. She was cross Ivan had deceived her. She pictured what his papa would do to him if he ever found out. Her response was to protect her son -

not from the school authorities, but from her husband's belt.

Should I tell Enrico? If I do, then Ivan will get the strap. If I don't, I'll be living a life of deceit and lies.

She held the letter close to her chest, wondering if she dared burn it.

I've never lied to Enrico, nor been deceitful. What would I say at confession? Oh! I've deceived my husband and saved my son.

Either way she sensed she was doing wrong. The strength of her love for Ivan was immeasurable, and the strength of her love for Enrico, unbroken. Following her conscience, she did what she thought best.

I'll confront Ivan and then tell Enrico I've dealt with the matter.

On telling Enrico, he went wild and wanted to take the belt to Ivan. She assured him that Ivan had fully grasped the implications of his truancy.

Having confessed, Ivan promised his mother he would never again play truant. The church confession was far easier than the reprimand from his mother. 'Hail Mary' said half-heartedly a few times was the price of forgiveness - an easy way out from his ill-conceived deceptions.

His mother's meeting with the head teacher proved fruitful. They agreed that whenever her son was absent from school without a note, the teacher would inform her.

Aware of the arrangement, Ivan feared shirking his lessons. He'd given his promise.

Antonietta was well used to spotting the tricks and antics of her offspring who tried to avoid school, especially on those days when subjects disliked were on the timetable. Ivan was as manipulative as his siblings in avoiding lessons. His mother knew the times he would feign illness, but like most mothers, she could not take the chance of sending him to school in case the illness was genuine.

Ivan was not exempt from the rigid rules of school punishment. During the post war era, corrective adjustment was the norm. A slap on the upper leg, a hard whack across the buttock from a baseball bat, a crack from a size ten sports shoe, or two to three strikes of a cane across the outstretched palm - held parallel for maximum effect - were but a few methods to enforce discipline. Whatever the punishment, some part of the anatomy suffered pain along with the loss of a little pride when tears flowed.

As time passed, the rest of Ivan's siblings were already seeking their own way in life. Only Laura and Ivan remained at home.

Money Maker

Ivan established his entrepreneurial drive long before adulthood. It seemed to be in his blood. Seeing an opening in the market, he scoured the streets and bombsites for scrap metal in exchange for cash. He built up a small amount of money and loved going to the pictures to see the latest films. With no idea how long the money would last, he had to be thrifty.

Of an age when girls had not quite caught his eye, cine films were his love. Such was his passion for the 8mm black and white home movies, he asked his papa if he could have a projector.

'Where do you think I can get the cash for such a thing? I've no money for luxuries.'

The answer did not quench Ivan's interest or longing. Some weeks later, Enrico arrived home carrying a package wrapped in brown paper.

'What is it?' asked Ivan as he, Laura and their mother eagerly gathered around the table.

Enrico ripped off the covering.

'A cine projector!'

Ivan was both thrilled and surprised.

Antonietta wondered how Enrico had bought such an expensive gift. Her inquisitiveness would have to wait at seeing Ivan excitedly plug the lead into the mains while his papa worked out how to fit the spool of film he had managed to acquire from the shopkeeper at no extra cost.

'It goes like this,' said Ivan taking the film from his papa and winding it through the gearing mechanism and shutter onto an empty spool at the rear.

'Here's a screen,' said Antonietta, pinning a white sheet on the wall.

The instruction book abandoned, Ivan switched off the lights and flicked on the projector. The family sat smiling as the three-minute black and white silent movie of Charlie Chaplin boxing a tough fellow flickered through the projector. Ivan hugged his parents for buying him something he had wanted for such a long time.

The short film showed signs of wear when his mother announced, 'It's time for bed, Ivan.'

'Just one more showing,' urged Ivan. The last showing of the night promptly followed. 'You'll have to let the lamp cool down, Papa, before packing it away.'

'I will. Don't worry. I'll be careful.'

Tucked up in bed, Ivan speculated on how he could buy more films.

When all was safely packed away, Antonietta posed the question she'd been longing to ask.

'How did you pay for Ivan's projector? It must have cost a lot of money.'

He looked sheepishly at her.

'I paid the shop keeper weekly. It's ours.'

He knew she disliked weekly payment plans. Hating debt, she believed in saving the money before handling the goods. She was pleased that Enrico had paid for the projector in full before bringing it home.

The following morning, Ivan invited his friends to the feature-length showing of the big film. The admission price of a lira paid in advance seemed a fair price. The first showing would be either a major success or one huge flop.

The premier showing was a triumph and value for money, as Ivan repeated the 3-minute feature several times without further cost to the clientele.

With money from his fledgling scrap metal business, and the cash from the admission fees, he added other 3-minute features to his collection. Not only was he astute in gathering in the cash, he had other ventures to try out. Knowing he could never beat the competition from the cinema up the road, he objected to paying a high price for a ticket and sought ways of reducing his costs.

The plan was simple. Standing in the foyer of the local picture house, he said innocently, 'One for the stalls, please.' Sitting at the front of the cinema, near the heavily curtained emergency door, he watched the adverts. Down went the lights. The feature film was about to be screened. Ivan was already at the emergency exit, pressing the handle.

'Shush! You have to be quiet.'

Soon his mates were with him, enjoying the film. The next time one of his friends paid to see the film, and the illegal entry continued. Occasionally he opened the large window in the toilet to let worthy friends scramble through. The practice continued for some time. Everyone except the proprietor was content with the arrangements.

Seated on the front row, the intruders were happily watching the big film when a light flashed into their eyes.

'Tickets!' bellowed an attendant.

Everyone fumbled in their pockets. Some made the excuse that they had lost them. Ivan was no exception. Seated on the end seat, he was easy prey for nimble fingers. Grabbed by his ear, he, along with his mates was ejected from the cinema. Their game was up.

The owner banned everyone from the picture house for months. As for telling his parents of his deceit, he decided not to mention the incident and hoped the cinema owner would keep his mouth shut.

When next in the confession booth confessing his misdemeanours, he said *Hail Mary* as many times as the priest instructed him to say without feeling guilty. It was just a part of life. The saying of a few words never hurt him, especially when absolved from his wrongdoing. Provided he attended church each Sunday and confessed regularly, he believed he was a good lad.

Fruitful Events

With his sparkling eyes and enduring smile, Ivan had developed a way of melting the strongest opposition. 'Ma, I'll be late home from school tomorrow. I'm going to Franco's house.'

'No you're not. You're to attend confirmation classes.'

'Must I, Ma? That's girls' stuff.'

'Of course you must. How will you get into heaven if you're not confirmed? You must attend, in preparation for your first communion. Classes start at half past four up at the convent. Don't be late. The nuns are expecting you. Your friends will be there.'

During his formative years, Ivan never gave God a thought. Religion was part of the fabric of life - something he did, rather than fully understand. It was a ritual of events to ease his conscience, offload responsibility and satisfy the adults. He was not pleased at having to attend lessons, but knew better than to challenge his mother.

After school, he trudged up the long drive to the convent with a few friends. He wasn't enthusiastic about learning the fundamental beliefs of the church he'd attended from childhood.

A high wall surrounded the house which was a huge stone building standing in its own grounds. A large reception area led off to the Mother Superior's office, kitchen, sitting rooms and a small quiet room where the nuns retreated for private prayer. A wide staircase accessed the nuns' sleeping quarters and bathrooms. The garden was crammed full with all manner of vegetables, soft fruit, apple, pear and plum trees. Shrubbery along with an abundance of flowers gave an array of splendid colour. The imposing front door stood like a prison gate. Ivan knocked hard, almost bruising his knuckles.

'Come in. My name is Sister Diorio, and you will address me as such,' fussed an elderly stern-faced foreboding nun.

In the hallway, she blurted out a number of instructions as if they'd come to stay.

'I forbid you to go upstairs. You are to observe quietness at all times, the exception being when asking or answering questions. You are to speak with dignity and in a soft voice. No outbursts of laughter, course joking or frivolity is tolerated. Anyone caught breaking the rules will be expelled and your family disgraced.'

A young nun joined her.

'This is Sister Fiorillo. She will help me with your studies. When you enter the sitting room, the girls are to sit apart from the boys. Is that understood?' Everyone nodded their understanding. 'Good! Then follow me.'

There were a few silent giggles behind the array of mocking faces, as the nun marched the little group into the sitting room to commence formal study.

'Sister Fiorillo and I shall tell you about our faith, the value of confession, the parables that Jesus told and the letters written by St Paul to the churches in Asia Minor.'

How much Ivan absorbed of the Bible truths at that time is conjecture. Certainly, his eyes and mind drifted off to the pretty girls and more so, the ripening strawberries he spied from the sitting room window.

Finding the older nun too stern and frightening, he preferred the younger one who was kind and gentle in nature. Her eyes shone with love. Even when Ivan and friends tested her patience, her tolerance and gentle response melted his heart, fixing deep within his memory the pleasure of her manner.

It was not all work. There were times when the candidates enjoyed the delights of the garden - especially when on one occasion the nuns were urgently called away, leaving the group alone.

'Come on,' said Ivan. 'Let's try the strawberries.'

The rest needed no encouragement, picking more than they could eat.

'What are you doing?' screamed an irate nun, running into the garden, her arms high in exasperation.

'Who gave you permission to take the fruit? You'll all pay for this!'

Just then, Sister Diorio returned with sister Fiorillo. 'What have you been up to?' she screamed.

The evidence clearly visible around their mouths and on their hands, the culprits bowed their heads low, more to hide their faces than in contrition.

'What will your parents say when they learn of your disgraceful behaviour?'

It was the first time they'd heard her shout. None thought she could be so boisterous.

'Please don't tell our parents,' said a brave little girl.

Sister Fiorillo looked at Sister Diorio, her glance full of compassion for the offenders.

'Possibly not,' she said, 'but you must promise never to steal again and confess your wrongdoing when next in church.'

There was a sombre nodding of heads. No one dared utter a word about the incident.

Confession cost the reciting of 'Hail Mary' 20 times as a penitence - a fair exchange for great-tasting strawberries and far better than a spanking.

Towards the end of the course, Sister Diorio announced excitedly, 'We are to take you on an educational outing to Rome.'

Ivan had never been to the capital and was as excited as the rest. The room quickly filled with banter at the prospects of seeing the sights.

'That's enough chatter,' said Sister Diorio. 'We've lots to discuss. We've been invited for lunch at our sister convent in Rome. I expect every one of you to be on your best behaviour. Do you understand? You are to be courteous to our hosts, saying 'please' and 'thank you' and smile when asking or answering questions.

'Politeness and good manners reflect who and what you are. None of your frivolity, Squillino!'

Ivan took exception to being singled out.

'Me?' I'm the best behaved here.'

This unfairness suppressed his concentration on spiritual matters. When walking home, he was quietly fuming at the injustice unfairly heaped upon him. An atmosphere of mutual and peaceful exchange was what he enjoyed, not confrontational remarks aimed at instilling insecurity and fear in a highly receptive developing mind. Eventually the hurtful remarks were confined to history, but like history, not forgotten.

Rome

The day trip to Rome had arrived. There was a buzz of excitement at the convent as kisses and farewells followed by flurries of parental advice scented the air. Boarding the transit van, the children were soon on their way.

Thirty minutes into the journey, Sister Diorio again warned the children sternly as to the consequences of misbehaving.

'And have a lovely time.' Sister Fiorillo added.

'We will!' came the collective reply.

On reaching Rome, Sister Fiorillo gave a running commentary as to what could be seen as they passed the various attractions of religious significance.

Sister Diorio was extremely pleased with the children's conduct as they walked through the city. The Colosseum and the Roman Forum were of exceptional interest to the boys. After a further walk, the transit van sped to the convent in time for lunch.

The building and grounds were more grandiose and spacious than those back home. Sister Diorio led the visitors into the vast vestibule where a number of resident escorted them into the dining room of long wooden tables and benches.

'We thought you'd like to sit here,' said one of the nuns pointing to a table next to the servery.

Everyone was enjoying the dessert when one of the boys flicked a spoonful of his pudding across the table. A quick response followed as another boy returned fire. Soon there was great laughter amongst the guests, including Ivan who joined in the fracas. The silence, now truly broken by loud giggles, Sister Diorio turned pink as every head turned towards the guests.

'Stop it! Stop it!' cried a resident nun. 'How disgusting! How dare you break our code of silence! Your manners are revolting.'

This outburst of censure caused the guests to giggle louder. At this, the nun seated at the head table stood in annoyance, shivered in disgust and sped out, leaving less responsible nuns to deal with the situation.

Sister Diorio jumped to her feet and sprang into action. 'How dare you abuse their hospitality by such unruly behaviour?'

The target practice immediately ceased, as did the exuberant giggles. The culprits fixed their eyes firmly on the table, fearing to raise their heads.

'Not only have you shamed Sister Fiorillo and me, you have shamed your family by this outrageous behaviour.'

'We've never had such an unruly lot as these,' said an elderly nun in disgust.

'Shameful. That's what it is. Shameful.'

Reluctantly, Sister Diorio agreed to continue the tour.

The van headed straight for Vatican City. Sister Fiorillo explained the background and history to the origins of St Peter's Basilica and the decorative Sistine Chapel.

Darkness was descending when they returned home.

Nothing was said about the incident in Rome. Ivan certainly kept his mouth shut when greeted by his mother.

No matter how many times 'Hail Mary' was confessed in penitence, Ivan felt no difference from entering the confession booth to leaving it. Even when in church, he felt no remorse when sticking chewing gum to the sole of those kneeling in prayer. To him it was just a bit of fun - something to laugh at with friends.

Going to church was something that everyone did. It was part of life. It was the way things were - the social fabric of acceptability within the community. It was unquestioned and never challenged. Church for Ivan was a place where his parents sent him, rather than inspiring a personal longing to attend.

Anxiety

Life for the Squillino family entered a phase where Ivan's parents could relax. From humble beginnings, they had struggled to provide a better life for their children. The older boys, working away from home, sent money to help the household budget.

All was well until an early morning disturbance awakened Ivan. Hearing anxious whispering coming from his parents' bedroom, he dashed to investigate. His sister was already there. Enrico sat upright in bed clutching his chest. The colour had drained from his face and droplets of sweat covered his brow.

'It's his chest. He's in pain,' said Laura. 'We've sent for an ambulance.'

'You fuss too much,' he gasped. 'I've told you. It's indigestion. I'll be fine.'

'That's what you say. I've lived with you long enough to know the signs of your so-called indigestion,' said Antonietta. She turned to Laura. 'When the ambulance comes, you are to stay here with Ivan. I'll be back as soon as I can.'

Enrico, suitably comfortable in a hospital bed, the long hours of tests and subsequent diagnosis took time.

Antonietta, seated in a corridor, waited anxiously for news. She'd enquired a number of times about her husband, but was told only that he was comfortable and that the doctor was with him. After a number of hours, a doctor approached her. 'Your husband has had a heart attack, Mrs Squillino.'

'Is it bad? Will he live?'

The doctor was non-committal. 'We'll keep him for a few days to monitor his progress. He is stable now.

We've done a few tests. We'll not know how badly his heart is damaged until the results are back.'

Antonietta spent some time with Enrico. He seemed content at being in the right place. The amyl nitrate tablet under his tongue had taken effect along with the morphine injection. He worried about Antonietta and the two back home more than he did for himself. 'You go and see to Ivan and Laura. I'll be fine. I don't want you worrying about me. Promise?'

'Of course I'll worry about you. You are my life. Don't ask me to promise. I have worried about you since the day we met and don't propose to stop now.' A touch of his old self appeared through his glazed eyes and ashen complexion. 'I love you.'

Antonietta held back her tears, praying for Enrico's recovery. They kissed and then she left. Enrico was her strength. Together they made a good team. She'd been the anchor holding the family together and he the foundation on which she stood. Now he was ill, she felt alone.

'How's Papa?' asked Ivan and Laura when she reached home.

'He's feeling much better,' she said, hugging her children to hide her anguish. 'I need to rest.'

Barely containing her emotions, she rushed upstairs to shed the tears she'd so bravely held back. Burying her head in a pillow to dampen the noise of her cries, she opened the floodgates of pent up sorrow. Clinging onto hope, she feared to think the worst.

Laura had not grasped the full seriousness of the situation. As for Ivan, he had little knowledge of what had gone wrong, yet felt the pain. He knew his papa was taking tablets for diabetes but never thought his heart would be a source of trouble.

After a few days, Enrico improved so much that a date was set for him to return home. Antonietta thanked God for her husband's recovery. Ivan also said a prayer for his papa.

Laura and Ivan were in the bedroom helping their mother prepare for Enrico's homecoming when Laura glanced from the bedroom window.

'That's strange. There's one of those telegram boys rushing up the path.'

'Let me see,' said her mother with hesitancy in her voice. Down the stairs they dashed.

'Special delivery,' said the messenger handing Antonietta an envelope.

Her heart sank on ripping open the seal. 'It's your Pa. He is gravely ill. I must go to him.'

'I'll go with you,' said Laura.

'No! You must stay with Ivan.'

'I'll be fine, Ma. Go with her Laura.'

'Don't let anyone in while we're gone,' she urged.

Ivan smiled. 'I promise, Ma.' Ivan waved the troubled souls off then uttered a prayer for his papa.

The short journey to the hospital seemed endless as costly seconds turned into lost minutes. The ward in sight, they rushed up the stairs, longing for Enrico to be well.

Breathless from the journey and hyperactive at the urgency, Antonietta approached a nurse.

'I'm Mrs Squillino. I've come to see my husband.'

The nurse's facial expression and body language conveyed everything she needed to say. A numbness filled Antonietta. Tears fell to Laura's cheeks as she comforted her mother.

'Come. You must sit awhile,' said the nurse. 'I'm afraid Mr Squillino passed away ten minutes ago. I'm sorry. We did all we could to save him. I'll make you a drink.'

In the alien environment of the hospital ward, for Antonietta had never been to a doctor or encountered the medical profession as intimately as on that day, she wept bitterly for her husband. He had been her protector, provider and best friend. Memories of the travesty at the loss of her first home, the experience of the convent, the rebuilding of their lives and the many happy times they'd shared, rumbled through her mind until the reality of her loss struck her like the force of a sledge hammer. Enrico was dead. Gone in an instant. Death had visited a second time. The first loss had been her three-year old son Antonio, and now her fifty-two year old husband.

Why

News of Enrico's death brought the family home. Ivan was barely 14 years old and at an age of questioning when his papa died. His happy demeanour was gone. A heavy cloud of sadness enshrouded him as he walked through the fields in search of a space to be alone. Speaking aloud, he questioned the futility of life. It was a time to challenge God.

'Why, God?

'Why did papa have to die? It's so unfair. Why take him from us just when life was becoming a little easier for him. He looked after us well. Why now? Why?'

Ivan believed in God. He knew Jesus had died on a cross, but had no knowledge of having a personal relationship with Him. In grief, he searched for an answer. It came through the one who grieved the most - his mother.

The funeral was a splendid affair. Almost all the village turned out to see the cortège and attend the church service as a sign of respect.

After the internment, Ivan sat on one of the benches in the church garden. He was still questioning God when his mother, sensing his hurt, came and sat beside him.

'I miss him, Ma.'

Tearfully he snuggled close to her, surrounded by an abundance of beautifully arrayed flora and gracefully leafed trees swaying in the warm, gentle breeze.

'Me too, Ivan.'

Her comforting arms enfolding him, the two sat in silence. He was searching for an answer as she relived the hardships and happy times they had shared.

'Why, Ma? Why did papa have to die?'

The question struck her deeply. What could she say? Through difficult family times she had struggled to ensure her children had had a good start in life. She'd been there for them in times of need and always had a positive answer to awkward questions. This time, words failed her. Unable to adequately express, explain or answer Ivan's question, her mind was blank. Tears filled her eyes as she absorbed the majestic display of God's floral creations.

'Do you see all these beautiful flowers and trees surrounding us?'

Ivan looked up.

'All these beautiful plants and trees were made by God so we can enjoy and take pleasure in their presence. If God gives us all these glorious treasures to make us feel well, who are we to deny Him having beautiful things in heaven? Heaven must be full of lovely things. Perhaps God takes those beautiful things from this world to make heaven more beautiful. Your papa was beautiful. I would like to think God took him to His garden to bring pleasure to those who see him. It comforts me to know that heaven is a beautiful place.'

Ivan hugged his mother tightly.

As the weeks slipped by, he came to accept the loss, but never forgot the love his papa had for all his children. Without a man to guide him in those formative years, a family friend took him under his wing. He let him sweep the floor and tidy his hairdresser's shop.

Within a year of Enrico's death, Ivan left school without qualifications and wondered what he would do. He was overjoyed when the family friend employed him to study hairdressing. Slowly, that inner glow that had once bubbled from the depth of his soul showed signs of renewal.

The hours were long, but the work was enjoyable. A five-hour stint between 8 a.m. and 1 p.m. brought a welcomed break until 4 p.m. closing at around 10 p.m. for six days a week.

He learnt a lot about life when listening to the local gossip and worldly chatter of the customers. Working hard in the salon and studying for his hairdresser diploma, there were however, times for leisure. During the summer months, the streets were active with shoppers, sightseers and revellers - a good reason not to rush home.

Joining his mates, he enjoyed the local festive atmosphere, walking the streets and spending time in the local coffee houses. Some nights it was well after 1 a.m. before he finally reached home to sleep what few hours remained.

No matter how late he returned home, his mother sat waiting for him. Frequently she had her head buried in her Bible. Often she would tell him, 'It's Jesus you need, Ivan. It's Jesus you need.'

Sadly, her advice fell on closed ears. A cursory smile, a gentle hug and Ivan would be off to bed, only to wake up tired and bleary-eyed. In contrast, his mother would be up early, praying at the church.

Reaching work by 9 a.m., Ivan would reap the harvest of his lethargy. The array of hairdryers working at full blast and the heat of the day added to his exhaustion.

He was not alone. His contemporaries also suffered fatigue. In contrast to the management work ethic, the employees' culture worked well. Unity prevailed. Each employee would in turn disappear to the toilet to nod off for ten minutes. A welcome respite for all concerned.

By the time he was 18, Ivan proudly held his diploma as a fully qualified hairdresser. Now the world was his oyster.

Enzo invited him to England to work with him and Sergio. His mother encouraged him to go. She loved him enough to know that opportunities rarely come twice in a lifetime. Had his sister lived away from home, Ivan would not have considered leaving his ma. Laura had met a local boy and would later marry.

Armed with the necessary work permits and documents, Ivan looked forward to working with his brothers in England. A word of caution from his mother took him by surprise.

'Now remember, Ivan. England is not Italy. They don't have the weather we have here. It gets cold at night. Enzo tells me it's not warm during the day either. You must keep warm, eat well, and take care of your health. Save your money and, above all, keep away from women. You'll always be poor if you bother with women. Find a good church to attend. I have told you more than once, it's Jesus you need. And don't forget to write.'

'I won't, Ma.'

'Won't what? Won't do any of these things I've warned you about?'

'No Ma. I'll do everything you say.'

Saddened at parting with her youngest child, Antonietta tried desperately to hide her sorrow and took comfort in knowing his older brothers would be there for him.

His mother was not alone in her loss. Since his father had died, his employer had treated Ivan as a son.

Ivan would miss his mother. Hugging her, he said his farewell. With no English, he headed for the airport, grateful to Enzo for having paid his fare.

New Prospects

The flight passed quickly. In England, he was on unfamiliar ground. Clearing customs, Ivan's reunion with Enzo and Sergio was heart-warming. The chatter about home continued with a plethora of Italian words filling the car as Enzo drove north. Ivan was curious and viewed with interest the varied landscapes, winding roads, towns and villages.

At home, the Mediterranean sun enhances the colours reflecting the varied shades of red on the rooftops and the diverse tones of stone buildings, both ancient and modern. His new environment of rows upon rows of uniform slate-roofed, brick built terraced houses, differed enormously.

A large industrial town was not what he'd pictured. Pungent smells of smelting furnaces hung heavy in some parts of the conurbation. He had come to England for a year and had to make the best of it.

Driving on the opposite side of the road proved strange and disorientating. Double-decker buses, a familiar sight to the natives, intrigued him, along with the diffused yellow glow from the night lights spaced along the street where he lived.

The food was a big change and the absence of a little wine at meals, a disappointment. Initially, Enzo ensured Ivan ate well and bought the occasional bottle of wine to remind him of home - not that he drank much. The wine was far too expensive to drink at every meal. Ivan soon learnt to go without. The local Chinese takeaway, cafes and reasonably priced restaurants proved to be winners.

After a few days' rest and keen to start work, Enzo took him along to the salon.

Enzo managed the salon of 25 chairs and 9 stylists. The shops belonged to an elderly couple of Jewish descent. The working hours gave plenty of time to absorb the nightlife Ivan had heard so much about.

The weekly wage of £8 was almost double to what a nurse received in those days.

The language barrier was overcome as Enzo was nearby to translate. Enhanced by his Italian accented English, Ivan became a great hit with his cheeky, playful character. The owners instantly took a liking to him and within the first week, raised his wage to £12. Within the year, his pay shot up to £18 a week.

Ivan enjoyed the banter with his clients. The tips showed how much he was loved by the female sector! After one year, he decided to stay.

Enzo was restless to start his own business.

Declining the offer of more money, he left with good grace.

Without the constant overseeing of his brother, Ivan was free to set his own goals. With his increased wage of £24, the Jewish couple treated him like family. He stayed there for a further four years.

He'd learnt how to smoke five to fifteen cigarettes a day and had tasted the beer. His body tolerated the cigarettes, but not the intoxicants. When drinking, he sensed a tightness in his throat as if being clamped shut. Alcohol was not for him. Whenever tempted to take a sip, the same frightening experience occurred. When sipping wine he would fall asleep.

A handsome, elegant and available Italian with his mother's words conveniently forgotten, he did not exclude love from his itinerary.

One female in particular caught his eye. Her long hair, beautiful face and shapely figure were a delight to behold. She sent shock waves through his body to such an extent that he shivered. Lacking the courage to ask her out, he saw her in a coffee bar and decided he could not restrain himself. He entered with a determination to fix a date.

He paused by her table. His legs wobbled. Losing courage, he sat at a distance from the young woman, occasionally raising his eyes to sneak a look.

'A large black coffee, please.'

Finishing his drink, he left feeling deflated.

Not long after that abortive experience, he saw her in a nightclub, looking more stunning than ever with her well-plaited hair. Supported by the seductive ambience of soft lights, music and tobacco smoke, he approached her. A number of girls sat with her.

'Would you like to dance?'

He tried to control his nervousness.

Muffled giggles erupted. Digging of ribs and eye fluttering were engaged at the sight of a slim, handsome Italian hovering around them. To the surprise of her friends, she stood and held his hand. From there on the relationship flourished. They met a few times a week before Ivan popped the question.

By now his brother had sold his hairdressing business and had opened an Italian restaurant. Ivan left his hairdressing job to help him. To enhance the restaurant's reputation, Ivan suggested introducing live music and the serenading of customers to bring an authentic atmosphere to the place.

He took guitar lessons to accompany his reasonable singing voice. Armed with a selection of chords and popular romantic melodies, he serenaded the clientele. His fame as the *singing waiter* soon spread.

Troubled Waters

Happily married, and the proud father of a lovely little girl, Ivan felt content - that was until Enzo phoned him.

'It's Ma. She's very ill in hospital.'

Ivan froze. 'What's wrong?'

'It's her water trouble again, and high blood pressure. She refused to see the doctor. Things worsened so Laura sent for him. I'm not sure how long she'll live.'

Enough said to convey the urgency, the call was brief. Within 24 hours the brothers were in Italy. Sadly, they were too late to say a final farewell. Their mother had died while they were airborne. With little to keep the pair in Italy, they were soon back in England. To suppress his grief, Ivan lost himself in work.

He continued serenading the clientele and visited a number of Italian restaurants in the area. A talent scout offered him a contract he could not refuse. He took his wife and daughter to London where he entertained in various high-class restaurants. Things worked out well for a couple of years but he eventually returned north with his family.

Seeing a gap in the market, he invested what money he had in opening an Italian restaurant. Securing premises in a prime position, he transformed the place. Planning, project managing, employing staff, advertising and overseeing the legal requirements associated with running such a business cost many hours away from his family.

Sadly, this affected the marriage. Separation and divorce followed.

As time passed, Ivan developed another relationship.

He sold his first restaurant and opened a second. Astute in business, he opened a hairdressing salon and a delicatessen shop next to each other. The flat above the restaurant provided full accommodation.

Ivan had everything materially he ever wanted in money, nice clothes and a Mercedes car. The businesses were booming until his partner announced she wanted to dissolve the relationship. His world collapsed. He'd been safe, secure and happy. Now he felt vulnerable, threatened and very much alone.

Low in spirit and confused in mind, his head battled with his heart, as reason and emotion struggled to find some clarity of understanding.

Desperate to find a way out of his embittered mind-set, he slipped deeper into a dark place of turmoil, turbulence and chaos. Once the soul of the party, the charisma he exuded had gone. Never before had he experienced so much trauma. Eager to escape, he phoned his brother Gino who was now living in Switzerland.

'Come and stay with my wife and me for a few days.'

Needing no encouragement, he arrived in Switzerland within days. The change of scenery gave him a much needed break from the day-to-day activities which had triggered his unrest. Chatting with Gino provided a way of expressing verbally how he felt - not so much offloading his problems onto his kin, but to hear aloud his own words and to clarify his thoughts.

A time to abandon his depressive mindset and reassess his life, Ivan loved walking in the mountains alone. He felt content and all seemed well, but lingering concerns were never far away.

He wrestled with dark emotions and irrational thoughts as he tried desperately to find some logic to his thinking. His mother's words echoed in his thoughts as he recalled her advice. *Keep warm, eat well, work hard, save your money and keep away from women!*

He'd certainly kept warm, eaten well and worked hard, as for the other two - he'd spent much and enjoyed female company.

By earthly standards, he knew enough not to dwell on past events, for when looking back there was a tendency to remember the regrettable and the bad things which had happened to him. The good things - the positives of life - were often second thoughts.

He was confused. *If I fail to recall my experiences, how can I protect myself against future events?*

Dwelling on regrets had led him to remorse and guilt which induced irrationality and self-destruction. He also knew that fixing his thoughts too much on the good things he had done could lead to overconfidence, self-importance and personal aggrandisement, which could also end in self-destruction. Within these variant extremes, he had to find a mid-course - a mode of behaviour acceptable to himself and others.

In such a frame of mind he found himself on the edge of a precipice, staring down into a valley of jagged rocks. In a moment of weakness, he heard demanding, destructive words.

Jump! Go on. Jump. I dare you. What's the point of struggling? You'd be better off out of it. Who cares about you? You're a nobody. Jump!

Alone on the mountain, he could feel someone pushing him forward.

Go on. Jump! Jump!

The taunting was relentless. A battle raged within him as the goading intensified.

Jump! Go on jump!

With the voice so real and the intensity so severe, it seemed so easy to escape reality and obey the taunts.

Life or Death

Ivan stared into the abyss.

Go on. No one cares about you. You'll not be missed. Jump!

The tempting voice dampening reason and rationality compelling him to submit. His step loosened, he edged himself closer to the edge. One sway and he would be gone. Irrationality reigned supreme.

Go on. Jump!

Gripped in a forward movement, a gentle breeze as if from nowhere kissed his cheeks, drawing him back to reality.

'You stupid man!' he cried out. 'What are you doing? Pull yourself together!'

Shocked at his near destruction, he sped with pounding heart to his brother's house, thankful to be alive.

Later pondering over events in his brother's sitting room, he half-heartedly scanned the array of books along the back wall. No reader, he now felt the urge to investigate. Fingering his way through the varied titles, a book written by N.V. Peale [1] caught his eye. Flicking through the pages, curiosity captured his imagination.

The more he read, the more he wanted to know. Engrossed in the book, he absorbed the words as they anchored to his mind and challenged his soul. His life's perspective renewed, Ivan took control. Well-rested, he returned to England with a far more positive attitude. His few days of respite had stretched to six weeks.

Resolving to make a fresh start, Ivan dissolved the partnership with the woman, and opened an Italian restaurant and a hairdressing salon in an adjacent town.

A more solemn demeanour took hold. His cliff edge ordeal well behind him, he was still not satisfied with his life. He knew something was missing. Unsettled, he sold both shops and managed an Italian restaurant for a friend. There he developed an insatiable desire to read the Bible. Why? He did not know.

During his 20 years in England, he'd gained a good command of the English language and possessed many of the dialectic pronunciations along with an abundance of idioms and local mannerisms. Despite this, he retained his Italian intonations. His adopted speech well-established, he lacked formal tutoring in English grammar.

The nagging desire to read an English Bible persisted.

Wandering through the local second-hand bookshops, he was delighted to find a child's illustrated Bible.

Recalling the parables the nuns had taught him, he read with enthusiasm about Jesus. His fear of reading sophisticated words fell into insignificance as the good news of Jesus Christ thrilled him.

A new love had touched him. Such immense joy filled his heart that he wanted to rush out and tell everyone the good news about Jesus. Alone in the quietness of his home, he was infused by God's love.

Like a hungry babe, he yearned for more of Jesus. Far from the land of his birth, he lacked the knowledge of what to do or where to go next.

---

1. *N. V. Peale, The Power of Positive Thinking.*

Eavesdropping

One particular evening, the restaurant he managed had been exceptionally busy. The employees were tired and longed for Ivan to lock the door.

'Good night,' said Ivan as the last customer left the restaurant. Suddenly two young men barged in.

'I'm sorry. We're closing,' said Ivan courteously.

'Please,' pleaded the elder. 'I've told my friend so much about how good the food is. I had to bring him.'

Conceding, Ivan escorted them to a table. The meal ordered and the drinks served, the elder of the two spoke freely and with much enthusiasm in his voice.

On hearing the name 'Jesus', Ivan eavesdropped on the conversation.

'You see,' said the man in a soft, melodic, Welsh accent, 'many Christians cling to religion rather than building a personal relationship with Jesus.

'The way I speak about him is as if Jesus were alive. Well, He is. Anyone who asks Him into their life can speak to Him - and more so - listen to His voice. Jesus walked this earth in the flesh. Now He is alive in the Holy Spirit.

'I'm speaking to you in the flesh. When I speak with Jesus, I speak to Him in the Spirit - God's Spirit. His Spirit is His gift to us, so that we can have fellowship with Him.'

'What do you mean?'

'Don't think me rude when I say there is a difference between hearing and listening. Sound is all around us but we don't consciously listen to each noise. We're selective. We hear only what we choose to hear.

'To hear Jesus, we need to listen. Jesus said that His sheep hear His voice (John 10:27). And they do. If we really want to hear Him - we will - even above the loudest of noises. It's about tuning in to His wavelength. I know He loves me, because He's told me so many times in word and through actions.'

The man had love in his voice, sincerity in his tone and enthusiasm in his manner. His heart, rather than his head, generated excitement. Each word conveyed God's love and faith in Jesus.

Ivan busied himself around the table listening intently.

'Your meals, Sirs,' said the waiter. 'Would you like parmesan?' The two nodded. 'Can I get you anything else?'

'No thanks,' smiled the talker. 'It looks delightful.'

Ivan was pleased when the man continued his conversation.

'Why people blaspheme God and curse Jesus when things go wrong in their lives is a mystery to me - especially those who deny God exists when things are going right for them. The big question is, does God exist or do we pray to the air? I know God exists. Jesus is as real as you or me.'

Ivan had heard people talk about Jesus, but never in this way. The terms, *alive and well, being with him, speaking in conversation just as any other person would* didn't seem real to him.

The sweet served, he hovered around the table, hoping to learn more of Jesus.

'If I could prove to everyone who doubts or disbelieves that God exists and that Jesus is alive, it would make the message of the cross ineffective. Each person needs to discover for him or herself if Jesus is real. Faith is the key and trust is the action. One step in faith is all it takes.'

'Can faith be defined?'

'When writing to the Hebrews the Apostle Paul said, "Faith is being sure of what we hope for and certain of what we do not see," (Hebrews 11:1).'

The two continued their dessert.

'Are you enjoying the food?' asked the enthusiastic believer.

'It's great. I'm glad you brought me.'

'You had to taste it for yourself to appreciate how good it is. Much like me telling you about Jesus. You have to taste Him for yourself to appreciate how great He is.'

Aware that Ivan had shown more than a skirting interest, on paying the bill the man asked, 'Do you know that Jesus loves you?'

Surprised, Ivan smiled and said nothing.

'Thanks for letting us in so late. It was good of you. My name is Andrew. You must visit my church one day.'

Time and directions confirmed, the two left.

The friendly invitation had touched him deeply. *Perhaps I'll visit. Perhaps not.*

The Best Friend

Ivan wanted more of the Heavenly Father he'd read about in his Bible - the Jesus he'd heard about when eavesdropping on the conversation.

An Italian in an adopted country, he had never entered a place of worship in England. He wondered what the service would be like. Would people welcome or ignore him? Not knowing what to expect, he pondered as to what he should do. Wanting more of Jesus, he asked himself, *What harm will it do if I go to church?*

As sure as night follows day, Sunday morning arrived. He'd worked late the previous evening and felt tired. Deciding to get up and go to church, he heard the words so plainly, *What are you going for? Stay in bed and go to dinner later.* It didn't take much for him to turn over in a warm bed and close his eyes. In a dreamy state, the man's words inviting him to church rang loudly in his ears. *I'll get up and go.* Those words soon had him out of bed, washed and dressed.

When driving to the place of worship, hesitation struck. *Do I go or not?* Parking the car, he sat wondering what to do. *I'm here now. I can't go home.* Doubt took hold as he approached the church entrance. *Shall I go in?* Many people were entering - young families, youths, elderly. Carried along with the flow, he found himself inside.

The church was not like the ones back home. It was just an ordinary building - more like a big hall than a church. Gingerly looking around, he saw no candles, icons, statues or confession booths. In contrast to the churches he'd visited, the place was alive with chatter.

A man with a beaming smile offered his hand.

'Pleased to see you. Is it your first visit?'

Ivan nodded and smiled nervously.

'You're very welcome.'

The congregation softened its chatter when a small group of musicians started playing. As words flashed up on a screen, everyone stood to their feet and joined in the singing.

Ivan thought they were all crazy when a number of worshippers swayed to the music, sang heartily and raised their hands in praise. He was, however, very moved by a young person with learning difficulties with raised hands singing his heart out in sincere worship.

It's real. It's real.

After the singing, someone stood up and spontaneously prayed, thanking Jesus and praising Him. Another stood up and said how God had spoken to him.

That's silly, thought Ivan. *How can God speak to him?*

Listening to the congregation sing again caused him to arrive at a decision.

If this is real, then I want it. This is what I'm looking for.

A leader of some kind took the floor.

'If you have your Bibles with you, please turn with me to Genesis 3 verses 1-10.'

Following the reading of the verses, the preacher looked directly at the congregation.

'Many of today's wisest thinkers consider what we've just read is fiction, concocted to satisfy the weak, and is irrelevant to modern society.

'Love is the reason God created the universe. Love is the reason God created you and me. This record enlightens us as to God's unfailing love and the foretelling of Jesus.

'The good news is that God's promise of salvation was accomplished at Calvary when Jesus hung on a cross.'

Twenty minutes into the sermon, Ivan sensed a deep inner stirring. He'd heard enough. He was up and away to his car to cry - not sorrowfully but joyfully. And cry he did. He could not wait to return the following Sunday.

It's real! Love filled the room. I felt it. It's real!

Over the following weeks, Ivan returned. He listened intently when the preacher spoke about a personal relationship with Jesus. At one point he felt a warm glow and sensed loving arms enfold him.

Things were different. Something had happened that brought joy and peace like never before. He wanted to tell everyone that he had met with Jesus. Infused with a new confidence, the charisma he had once enjoyed return with renewed vigour. He began to courageously read an adult version of the Bible. He took comfort in these words:

For the message of the cross is foolishness to those who are perishing, but to us who are being saved it is the power of God.

The words leapt from the page as he kept reading.

I will destroy the wisdom of the wise; the intelligence of the intelligent I will frustrate. Where is the wise man? Where is the scholar? Where is the philosopher of this age? Has not God made foolish the wisdom of the world? For since in the wisdom of God the world through its wisdom did not know him, God was pleased through the foolishness of what was preached to save those who believe (1 Corinthians 1:18-30).

Absorbing the truth, his lifestyle was about to change.

From Smoke to Fire

Ivan lived in clean surroundings. He loved to look spotless and healthy. He enjoyed pleasant things around him - free from pollutants. That said, he had a problem that caused him concern. He enjoyed a cigarette.

Since meeting Jesus, he'd read about the body being described as *'the temple of the living God'*, *(2 Corinthians 6:14-17)*.

Not wanting God's Spirit to live in a body full of nicotine, he longed to stop smoking. No matter how he tried, the habit of 20 years remained a problem. His working environment encouraged an atmosphere of friendliness and relaxation where cigarettes were part of the social scene. Recognising the tight hold of smoking was easy in comparison to kicking the habit. He prayed earnestly that God would help him abstain.

Three months had passed since his original prayer as he continued to inhale the poisonous gases.

It was not by chance, coincidence or fate that he stopped smoking. Neither did it come by some striking revelation or the immobilising of his arm that prevented him from lifting a cigarette to his lips. His answer came through a regular seasonal event. He caught a severe cold resulting in a nasal infection. Not willing to suffer further bouts of self-inflicted pain, the decision to stop smoking was ultimately his. Nicotine free, he pursued a deeper relationship with Jesus.

Some time later, a baptismal service was arranged for those who'd invited Jesus into their lives.

Baptism was not for Ivan. He'd been christened as a baby and saw no reason to - in his words - *be done again.*

'Have you thought about being baptised?' asked the pastor.

'I was baptised when a baby.'

The pastor smiled knowingly.

'Baptism is different from christening.'

'What do you mean?'

'It was your parents' decision - not yours - to have you christened as a baby. There are many reasons why you should consider going through the waters of baptism.'

When Jesus was a babe in his mother's arms, she presented Him to the priest. Jesus was baptised by total immersion in the River Jordan. Just before His ascension into heaven, He said these words:

"Go into all the world and preach the good news to all creation. Whoever believes and is baptised will be saved, but whoever does not believe will be condemned. And these signs will accompany those who believe: In my name they will drive out demons; they will speak in new tongues; they will pick up snakes with their hands; and when they drink deadly poison, it will not hurt them at all; they will place their hands on sick people, and they will get well," (Mark 16: 15-18).

Ivan did not fully realise the significance of his reply when he said, 'If that's what Jesus wants, then I'll do it.'

There were 12 candidates for baptism at the local swimming pool. Just before each baptism, the pastor read out a Bible passage as an encouragement to the one being baptised. The Bible verses for Ivan read:

Since, then, you have been raised with Christ, set your hearts on things above, where Christ is seated at the right hand of God. Set your minds on things above, not on earthly things. For you died, and your life is now hidden with Christ in God. When Christ, who is your life, appears, then you also will appear with him in glory, (Colossians 3:1-4).

As the weeks rolled by, his exuberant, flamboyant manner increased in proportion to the love he found in Jesus. His 'banana smile' projected his wholesome, happy character.

Since the day he had invited Jesus into his life, he'd risen around 4 a.m. to speak with Jesus. Not long after his water baptism, he was in his kitchen praying, when suddenly, a strong gust of wind filled the room. Pots and pans shook. Ivan dropped to the floor as God's Spirit touched him. He lay there for some time, enjoying the Presence of God. This was truly a Pentecostal experience.

In the restaurant one day a customer asked, 'What's happened to you?'

'How do you mean?'

'You're different.'

'It's Jesus.'

Ivan enthusiastically told him about the change Jesus had brought. On another occasion a friend invited Jesus into his life. Rushing home to tell his wife the good news, she was not impressed.

'It's a fake. It won't last,' she said sceptically.

Contrary to her belief, the man's excitement and love for Jesus grew stronger each day. He stopped smoking and gambling. His wallet became heavier and his health improved.

Curious to know what spell, influence or fakery he'd come under, his wife tested the waters by going with him to church.

Fired up to tell the world about Jesus and God's salvation, such was Ivan's desire to tell everyone that Jesus loved them, his customers were not exempt. He took every opportunity to talk about Jesus. Many customers asked Jesus into their lives and Ivan was quick to invite them to worship Jesus at his church.

The restaurant owner expressed concern when the place filled with believers.

'Your enthusiasm may disturb business.'

Ivan gave him a big smile. 'Don't worry. If the business fails we'll open a church!'

Prison Beckons

Not long after receiving the promised Holy Spirit, Ivan went to prison, but not for any misdemeanour. Giving no second thought to the matter, he agreed to befriend an inmate. Spiritually alive in Christ, he soon experienced the tensions, concerns and unsettling emotions at the thought of entering such an establishment. He'd seen films about the notorious Alcatraz in San Francisco Bay and Robben Island, South Africa, but had never been inside a Victorian stone built house of correction with its high, foreboding granite walls, iron gates and long slated roof and cellblocks with their small, barred windows.

Ivan was nervous when passing through the many security checks, searches, frisks, metal detectors, barred doors, and constantly being watched by cameras and prison guards. That was to get in! Getting out was much harder. His anxiety, fear and uncertainty soon left when considering his visit was an opportunity to tell the man about Jesus and perhaps lead him to Christ.

The first meeting went well. Later, the prison chaplain invited Ivan to help in the services. Depending on the reasons for detention, and more so to safeguard Ivan, the custodians only allowed him to play his guitar. At other times, they let him use the public address system. Many prisoners accepted Jesus as their Saviour.

Things were going well when suddenly, the authorities transferred the evangelically motivated prison chaplain to another prison. The doors were firmly shut to any further evangelistic activity.

Such was Ivan's longing for others to experience the love Jesus brings that God led him to Market Place

Evangelism. He loved telling people how he came to know Jesus and invited many to church. Christmas and Easter were the most active times. Asking questions such as, 'Is Jesus relevant today? Do you believe in Jesus' Resurrection?' made people think.

On other occasions, he undertook local surveys about the area and its likes and dislikes. He would ask about life in general, including employment and spiritual welfare. The Lord had prepared him well for his future role.

Dependable and accepted by others, his roots in the Italian markets came in useful. A frequent visitor to his local market, he still takes every opportunity to talk to the stallholders about their spiritual wellbeing. A true evangelist at heart, nothing detracts or deters him from reaching others with the love of the Lord Jesus.

Along with others he has held evangelistic classes in schools, rest homes and coffee bars. He has conducted school assemblies using music and mime to explain the gospel. He has entertained with tricks to capture attention and make the children laugh.

To finance himself he started home-hairdressing and spent time working in residential homes for the elderly. Whether picking up a pair of hairdressing scissors, a waiter's tray or a guitar, Ivan's eagerness to serve his Saviour has always been uppermost.

Words became actions when inviting anyone to church. Having invited a friend who lived in a residential home for people with physical disabilities, others also wanted to attend. Not wishing to disappoint, Ivan learned to drive their minibus.

One day, his brother Enzo asked him to help in his restaurant. This he did on a part-time arrangement.

Enzo didn't know what he'd let himself in for as Ivan continued much as he'd done previously. Enthusiastically, he told customers of Jesus' love. Such was his determination to share the gospel with others, a customer asked, 'What you've shared with me tonight - will you repeat on the local radio?'

Ivan was delighted and agreed.

Seeing an opportunity to publicise the restaurant, Enzo joined his brother.

Speaking of the love and joy Jesus had brought to his life, Ivan, with his immutable 'Amigo' debonair style, played his guitar while singing songs he had written. The first entitled *'How wonderful to know you really love me,'* tells of what Jesus means to Ivan.

> *How wonderful to know you really love me*
> *How wonderful to know you really care*
> *How beautiful to feel your arms around me*
> *Filling my heart with so much love and so much care*
> *How beautiful to feel sunshine and laughter*
> *That fills my empty heart with love divine*
> *To share this life with you now and forever.*
> *How wonderful to know you really love me.*

His second song tells of the love, peace and joy of knowing Jesus.

> *I can remember when I was without you, Lord.*
> *Looking for a love I could not find.*
> *Seeking for a peace that the world cannot give,*
> *And you came into my life and gave me love.*
> *Gave me love, gave me peace and gave me joy,*
> *And your love endures forever, evermore.*
> *You never leave me nor forsake me, Lord.*
> *How wonderful to know,*
> *You're my king, you're my Lord, you're my Father.*
> *When I think about who you are,*
> *You created the heavens and the earth,*
> *The moon, the sun, the stars, the seas and the trees*
> *Almighty God you are, yes you are.*
> *You're my king, my Lord, you're my Father.*
> *How I love to raise my hands and praise your name.*
> *You never leave me nor forsake me, Lord.*
> *How wonderful to know,*
> *You're my King, you're my Lord, yes, you're my Father.*

Following the radio slot, he received a request to speak at the Full Gospel Businessman's Fellowship. A cooked breakfast followed by lots of tea and toast, set the scene in one of the local hotels. Many more public speaking invitations followed for him to talk of how he'd met with Jesus. The gospel had to be shared and Ivan never missed an opportunity.

Trust

Ivan had had his share of psychological and physical trauma. Since meeting Jesus however, he'd been exceptionally well. He maintained a wholesome diet, exercised regularly and was nicotine free. He was in church when someone asked him to pass them a book.

Reaching to grip the book, Ivan cried out in pain.

'What's wrong?' asked the alarmed woman.

'It's nothing. Just a twinge in my back.'

He forgot the incident until it struck a second time. Painkillers, hot water bottles, heat pads nor anti-inflammatory creams brought little relief. Such was the intensity of the pain he visited his doctor who shook his head despairingly. His depressive look sowed seeds of hopelessness.

'It's degenerative. Your condition is incurable. You'll be in a wheelchair within a few years.'

Dreams and aspirations shattered, Ivan was devastated. He pictured himself alone, confined to his house. The outcome defined, the consultation abruptly ended with negative thoughts plaguing him. His mind in chaos, he returned to his car.

Turning the ignition, a spurt of defiance suddenly erupted.

'No! No! I'll not accept the doctor's prophecy! I belong to Jesus. He has things for me to do. I refuse any disability. Heal me, Jesus. Heal me!'

Faithful to His word, Jesus answered.

'Ask and it shall be given unto you. Seek and you will find. Knock and it shall be opened onto you,' (Matthew 7:7).

The back pain subsided and eventually left.

Sometime later, a female evangelist from Australia visited the church. After the services, she invited Ivan and a pastor to help with a healing crusade on the west coast of England. The event would last for seven days. He was thrilled and looked forward to sharing the gospel.

He could only be absent from work for three days and had to finance himself. Not knowing what to expect, off he went to tell others how he had met Jesus.

Each morning the evangelist rose at 4 a.m. to pray until 7 a.m. before leading the morning worship. In the evening, she prayed for the sick. Numerous people accepted Jesus as their Saviour and many were healed.

After an active evening service, the evangelist surprised them with an unexpected announcement.

'I won't be here tomorrow night. I'm taking the night off.'

The pastor's raised voice and agitated words aptly expressed his disapproval.

Reaffirming her decision, she added, 'I have to do what God wants me to do. Ivan can pray for the sick.'

Swallowing hard, his throat felt clogged. This would be the first time he'd ever prayed publically for anyone.

Ivan felt nervous as the congregation gathered. In the quietness of a sanitized room, he knelt and prayed, asking God to fill him with what He would have him say.

Over 300 people were in the church when the musicians led the congregation in worship. After the pastor's short talk, Ivan spoke of how he'd met Jesus. Those requesting prayer for healing were invited to the front. Many came forward.

Ivan prayed silently, trusting Jesus would answer. As each person approached him, he breathed on them and prayed for their healing.

An unruly woman stepped forward exhibiting an evil spirit. Standing firm in faith, he commanded in the name of Jesus that the demons depart. Down to the floor she fell, rolling about in anguish. Moments passed as peace took hold. She lay there calm and serene. After some time, she stood to her feet. Praising Jesus, she walked away rejoicing.

Many abandoned their walking sticks and asthmatics were relieved. Ivan never doubted the power of God who faithfully answered prayer.

Questions remained. 'Why did the evangelist walk out at such a critical time? Why did she leave Ivan to pray for the people? Not until after the evening service did the reason become clear. By directing the evangelist to walk away from the situation, God opened the way for Ivan to fulfil the work God wanted him to do. From then on, his faith and healing ministry grew.

In church one Sunday morning, someone tapped Ivan's shoulder. It was the woman who had followed her husband to church, keen to pour scorn and contempt on his belief the moment he abandoned God.

'I'm ready to invite Jesus into my life.'

Smiling hesitantly, she spoke softly. That moment, another great adventure had begun, as the angels in heaven sang praises to God. Such is her love for Jesus, she too now spends her time telling others of His love.

Ivan continued to work at the restaurant, serving customers and telling what Jesus had done for him. He wasted no time in sharing the Good News of Jesus with a young couple who visited the restaurant. Seemingly interested in what he had to say, Ivan invited the young man to church. Although he asked Jesus into his life, it became evident that he had many issues. Befriending him, Ivan worked hard to ease the troubled soul. Weeks passed into months and then he stopped attending church. A phone call caught Ivan unawares.

Family

'Have you heard the news?' asked a friend.

'What news?'

'The young man you befriended. He's dead.'

Ivan went cold. Nothing more was said.

The funeral was a sombre event as relatives and friends, struggling with their emotions, gathered on a cloudy, wintry day around the graveside. Having met the man's parents previously, glances of condolence and acknowledgement crossed the open grave between him and the family.

A young woman he assumed was the sister of the deceased looked his way and then continued her grieving. Ivan had gone to the funeral out of respect and if possible, to comfort family members in their hour of need.

Of Indian descent, Daphne had arrived in England when eight years old with her parents. An attractive woman of medium height she had flowing black hair and deep brown eyes. Forthright, honest and strong in persuasion, she possessed a softness of heart.

Life had not been kind to her, and like many who seek happiness in this world of turmoil, she had tried hard to make sense of her life. Brought up in the religion to which Ivan had once subscribed, ritual and weekly confession was not for her. When 11 years old, she had attended the Salvation Army, but as time passed, her faith waned.

Well before the funeral, Daphne's sister had married a police officer. He'd listened to two Mormons express their faith. Unimpressed, he'd heard enough to pick up a Bible and examine the contents. What he read touched his heart. He invited Jesus into his life.

Initially, his wife was not pleased. Seeing the change in her husband, she was motivated to ask Jesus into her life.

Phoning Daphne one evening, the conversation moved onto spiritual matters.

'It's Jesus you need. You ought to go to a church.'

Daphne listened with interest and eventually decided to give church a go. She visited a number of churches, but none seemed to possess that 'something'.

While visiting a friend one day, she picked up a leaflet inviting people to a Gospel Outreach.

Harbouring apprehension, yet keen to discover what it was all about Daphne went along. A warm welcome awaited her as friendly greetings allayed her anxiety. When listening to the gospel message, she felt it was solely for her. Not long after her first visit she asked Jesus fully into her life. Never before had she felt His arms around her so lovingly. From that moment, she knew without doubt that Jesus was alive and that He loved her with an everlasting love.

There would be no turning back.

Daphne's faith and knowledge of Jesus grew. Reading her Bible was a pleasure rather than a chore.

Occasionally church friends invited her out for a meal. Sadly, when arrangements were finalised to indulge in fine cuisine, due to pressing commitments, Daphne, couldn't go. There was always a willing tongue to describe the meal and more so, the handsome Italian waiter who constantly spoke of his love for Jesus. The restaurant with its good food and the charm of this Italian, was always a favourite watering hole for Daphne's friends.

Following the funeral, Ivan offered his help to console and look out for the family. He enjoyed the family environment and sensed a fondness for Daphne.

Never stepping out of line, he struggled with his intensifying admiration of her. However, it was important that her love for Jesus was as deep as his own love for his Saviour.

Everyone was surprised when she turned up at church with the handsome Italian waiter. The pair looked good together and comfortable in each other's company.

His love for her deepened but he continued to hide his feelings. Even when their eyes met in those intimate moments when words are silent and minds active, he held back from saying anything, committing those few pleasurable seconds to his heart.

What had started as an encouraging word in tragic circumstances had moved on beyond a platonic friendship to real love. Ivan agonised over whether to tell her his true feelings. From the way she looked at him, he knew she liked him a lot. It was make or break time. He prayed frequently about the relationship. With his love for her increasing, he hoped that she too felt something for him.

'I need your advice,' he told a friend.

The church leader was keen to listen.

'I think I'm falling in love. No! I'm sure I've fallen in love.'

'Is she a Christian?'

'She is.'

'Do you love her?'

Ivan's answer beamed from his face. 'I do.'

'Then what's the problem?'

'There isn't one.'

'Then what are you waiting for? Marry her!'

Ivan never expected such a direct answer. Off he went to seek God's blessing, before bubbling out the content of his heart to Daphne. He was shaking when he approached her.

'What's wrong?' she asked.

'Nothing.' Unable to contain himself, his words sounded more serious in tone than intended.

'I want to love you but I only want to serve the Lord. Please don't think me rude when I say Jesus comes first in my life. I can have no greater love than for Him. If you can live with that and agree to let Him direct our lives as He does mine, then without hindrance or question, I offer my love, such as it is, to you.'

Daphne was silent, and then responded.

'I know just how you feel. I too love Jesus. Whoever falls in love with you will have to be second best.'

Ivan smiled. 'You know what I mean. I've come too far with Jesus to give Him up now. He's my best Friend and always will be. Please don't take this the wrong way. I cannot love anyone who blocks my relationship with Jesus, or acts as a stumbling block to the things He wants me to do and the places He directs me to go.'

Daphne did not hesitate. 'I accept your offer.'

Prospective In-laws

Some weeks later, Daphne's parents invited Ivan to dinner. Although they had met briefly, it would be different as a prospective son-in-law.

'Come in!'

Daphne's mother ushered Ivan into the front room. Her radiant smile, soft brown eyes, black hair and bronze complexion highlighted her warm personality.

'Make yourself comfortable,' she said, offering him a seat. Daphne vanished into the kitchen to find her dad.

'I'll put the kettle on. My husband won't be long. He's out at the back mending the clothes line.'

In walked a casually dressed, slimly built, six-feet two inches tall man, wearing a roughly woven flat cap. Ivan moved to stand.

'Don't get up on my account.'

With a broad smile and a firm handshake, he greeted Ivan.

'It's a while since we met.'

Cordial conversation followed as Daphne and her mum walked in with a tray of teas and coffees.

Ivan addressed his prospective in-laws courteously as Mr and Mrs Soraine. Never once did he use their first names.

A strong-willed individual, Mr Soraine had been born into a world of civil unrest the year Mahatma Gandhi became leader of the Indian National Congress. Of French and Irish descent, his demeanour was jovial with a touch of fearlessness.

A practical man, he could put his hand to anything. Mr Soraine was 14 years old when he started his formal education. His determination to make something of himself drove him to study hard. Mostly self-taught, he worked hard and gained a trusted position as a supervisor with the Indian Railway system.

During his time working with people of numerous languages, he acquired the ability to speak several fluently and had a smattering of two others.

Mrs Soraine, although weak in body due to a debilitating illness, was likened to Ivan's mother in being prayerful, sincere, gentle and exceptionally kind. She loved cooking. A good curry was a highlight for visitors.

As has been said, Ivan never missed an opportunity to tell others about Jesus. Daphne's parents were not exempt. Nominal worshippers, they held the faith of ritual and confession.

Meeting the potential in-laws proved successful. They liked her choice - not that she needed their approval. She was of an age to decide for herself.

At this point, Daphne had not yet been baptised by total immersion. Trusting Jesus, she made the arrangements at her local church and was thrilled that her parents witnessed her baptism. Ivan was delighted.

The wedding proceeded without hindrance, and with Jesus at the centre to direct and guide their every step, the pair embarked on their new life together - Daphne as Ivan's earthly rock, and Jesus their spiritual.

A Wider Mission

Ivan has continued to tell the gospel message with love, enthusiasm and compassion. God opened the way for Ivan and Daphne to share the gospel with her parents.

They later received a call from Mr Soraine.

'You know what we've been talking about? I'm ready.'

The pair immediately drove to his house and prayerfully shared their joy when both parents asked Jesus into their lives and to be baptised.

After preaching one Sunday, a tall, well-dressed Kenyan introduced himself with a firm handshake.

'I'm Pastor Joseph. While you were speaking, the Lord told me to invite you to Kenya to preach at various churches. So here I am, inviting you to Africa. The people back home would love you to share the gospel with them.'

The invitation came as a surprise. Eager to stay in God's will, he smiled and gently said, 'Well, the Lord has not told me! I need to ask him.'

The answer came by way of a deep sense of need to share the gospel. Financing themselves, Ivan contacted Pastor Joseph and the preparations for a full evangelistic programme got underway.

When Ivan and Daphne arrived at the airport prior to departing for Africa, a man was waiting to see them. 'While praying this morning, the Lord told me to give you £200.'

Grateful that the Lord had seen their need and provided a little extra for the visit, they thanked the man for his kindness.

Africa was new to them. Nothing had prepared them for such heat when landing at Nairobi. After passport control, and a hearty welcome from Pastor Joseph, a six-hour car journey lay ahead.

Sweat, dust, bumpy uneven roads and an absence of air conditioning in the car added to the visitors' discomfort. Not knowing what facilities would greet them, Ivan, commented, 'All I want right now is a long refreshing soak in a hot bath.' He glanced at Daphne. She said nothing.

'There's a shop not far ahead,' said Joseph. 'We'll stop for a break. Would you like a chicken sandwich?'

'That would be great,' smiled Ivan, picturing delicious tender slices of freshly garnished chicken with thinly sliced tomatoes, wrapped in soft, newly baked bread.

Reaching the small oasis, tired, stiff, hot and sweaty, the two stretched their legs to ease the cramp, while Joseph went to buy sandwiches. Ivan said nothing when handed a hard bread role with an equally solid piece of chicken. He wondered whether to chew the chicken, swallow it whole or make a bouncy ball from it.

This was the real world of privation. He was witnessing at first hand the joys and hardships of living in a land that had everything, but remained poor.

Arriving at a remote village, the longing for a bath faded into insignificance when handed a bucket of water.

Despite the lack of modern amenities, the people they met had a love and a joy that shone as any star.

The first church was no more than an elongated mud building with a corrugated tin roof. Seated on rows of low, rickety wooden benches were almost 60 people.

Material things became of little importance as the congregation sang, swayed and danced their hearts out.

The first evangelical meeting was a great success as God's Presence clearly filled the room. Each thanked and praised God that He'd heard their prayer and sent them an evangelist.

Journeying to another village, there was great activity in a large, dry and dusty open area where blades of grass struggled to break through the parched land. Locals were busy knocking together a makeshift platform with anything to hand. When finished, it was nothing more than planks of wood on two trestles with an iron bar at waist height to steady those daring to venture onto the structure. Of precarious construction, perhaps prayer held it together during the service! It needed to support at least 12 people singing and swaying to the music provided by guitar players, their voices amplified by a single microphone and a small black box. An almost clapped-out generator provided the electricity.

Hundreds of people gathered around the platform, standing inquisitively to hear what Ivan would say. Many excited, ill-clad, barefooted children of all ages stood amazed as to what was happening. When the music resounded around the wide-open area, the children danced to the melodies as the platform party sang gospel songs.

Ivan preached with his usual sincerity and a touch of urgency - eager to encourage others to invite Jesus into their lives.

As dusk approached, many responded and came forward for prayer and healing.

Working Together

After preaching for three days, Ivan was looking forward to relaxing. His throat was feeling sore and the dry air didn't help. By the time his rest day came, it felt as if it was coated with sandpaper. Praying for healing, he spent his day-off in bed. Sleep was gratefully accepted as the heat faded and the cold night air slipped silently across the land.

Drifting into a light slumber, he pictured the beauty of the country. His dreaming took on a more serious tone with what God showed him. He later delivered the message of the dream to the organisers.

'God has shown me a spirit of competition amongst you. He says if it does not stop, He will not bless you.'

Everyone was shocked that he knew of their differences. Ashamed of how they'd conducted themselves and sincerely repentant, a unison of spirit prevailed. From there on, God blessed them as He released His power. The attendance increased tenfold from 200 to 2 000. Many souls invited Jesus into their lives.

Ivan and Daphne travelled many miles, sharing the gospel message with thousands. After a few days' respite, they entered the wilderness to meet the Maasai people. Kenya was suffering a severe drought at that time and on entering a Maasai village, they were sad that the men were not there. They had taken their cattle in search of water.

The village was a small, circular, dusty compound surrounded by equally dry twigs, brushwood and shrubbery. Enclosed were numerous small, rounded mud huts with thatched rooves.

Ivan saw that the Maasai lived starker lives than he had seen on film. Two women, one nursing a baby in her arms, greeted the visitors; no ritual dress of colourful material and highly decorative sparkling bracelets here. They wore plain blue sleeveless dresses, with thin plastic belts around their waists. Single threaded necklaces and bracelets dangled from their necks and wrists. A thinly woven material of dull red patterned squares was draped over the shoulders, secured by a loose knot across the breast. They were barefooted with shaven heads. Five sparsely dressed children - four of them under six years of age - joined the women. Despite their lack of material possessions, the women and children carried a peace that outshone their depravity.

Ivan was thrilled when the interpreter told him that they knew Jesus as their Saviour and read the Bible in their native tongue.

The women sang a melodious gospel song, clapped their hands and praised God. The visitors joined in the worship, thanking God that He had brought them there - and more so - that the Maasai loved Jesus.

Before departing, they received many invitations to return to meet the men. Sadly, time did not permit. Their time in Kenya conducting evangelical and healing meetings a success, time had quickly passed. Ivan and Daphne returned home.

A few months later, Joseph was in England and stayed with Ivan and Daphne for a few days before returning home via London. While there, Joseph scribbled a list of items he wanted to take back to Africa and then announced, 'Today I'll pray and fast for these.' Believing he would receive everything he needed, he placed the list on the hall table and then locked himself in his room to pray. From the moment he closed the door and knelt to pray, the phone started ringing.

Ivan tentatively glanced at the list: *electric guitar, sound system, microphones, generator, a set of drums* and much more. By nightfall, God had provided everything on the list with the exception of a set of drums.

'The Lord will provide,' said Joseph confidently. 'My time here is not yet over.'

Joseph arranged transportation of the things he had asked God for and headed for London, confident he'd need to add a set of drums to the shipment. While in London, a man who knew nothing about Joseph's prayer, approached him.

'My son has a set of drums that he no longer plays. He wondered if you would like to have them.'

Joseph smiled knowingly, praising God for His great provision. The list was complete.

Jesus said: *I tell you the truth, my Father will give you whatever you ask in my name. Until now you have not asked for anything in my name. Ask and you will receive, and your joy will be complete,* (John 16:23-24).

Joseph took God at his word. Believing He would answer his prayer, he put faith into action and God was faithful to him.

Three months later, Ivan returned to Africa with a colleague and stayed for two weeks, visiting over 15 churches. Before departing, he bought rolls of film to take with him. When buying the film, the manager handed him a set of watches.

'What's this?' he asked.

'They're free with the film. It's an offer we're running. You'd best take them. The offer is about to end.'

'Thanks, I'll give them to the folks in Africa.'

In Africa, many came to listen to Ivan and invited Jesus into their lives. On one day in particular, he visited an isolated area of scattered villages. He'd arrived with Joseph at a village comprising three houses, one shop and a generator. While there, Joseph asked Ivan to conduct a funeral. Everything was going well until the relatives and friends gathered around the grave. Ivan was praying at the graveside, when a man nursing his jaw nudged him.

'I'm in pain. Will you pray for my tooth?'

Turning to the man, Ivan prayed for his healing.

'My pain has gone!' the fellow yelled.

The minor disturbance at an end, the funeral service continued as if nothing had happened.

News of the miraculous event travelled fast throughout the surrounding villages. Almost everyone from the district came for prayer. Many received healing.

The Wheel

Back home, at the end of a busy schedule, Ivan longed for a good night's sleep. He'd been in bed for some time when, in a dreamlike state, he saw a white cloud above him. The cloud slowly cleared, revealing a huge wheel hovering above him. Staring hard at the wheel, its spokes and central hub were clearly visible. Slowly, the wheel descended. Closer and closer it came, pressing him into the mattress.

Beset with anxiety, he struggled to escape. The wheel pressed against his face, chest and abdomen. The weight bore down heavily upon him. His chest tightened. Unable to move, and thinking he was about to die, the pain intensified, as if at any moment his heart would burst.

He struggled to breathe. He tried to wake but could not. Suddenly, the wheel vanished, along with his pain. He awoke clutching his chest, agitated and trembling.

Not knowing the significance of the traumatic event, and unable to sleep, he prayed the night hours away.

On rising, he told Daphne his dream. The interpretation evaded her.

On telling a friend of his vivid experience, the man sat thoughtfully.

'Lots of people have dreams. Not every dream has a meaning. Our heads are bursting with so many things. Sometimes our minds get muddled, especially when in sleep.'

'My mind was not muddled. The dream was so clear.'

'I don't doubt it. Perhaps you should wait for confirmation to see if this wheel is important. I'd be inclined to think of it as one of those muddled occasions and forget it.'

Ivan was not convinced, but understood his friend's logic.

The dream having been so vivid, he decided to wait for some revelation or spiritual word from a secondary source that would reveal its meaning.

On another occasion, Ivan was praying with his eyes firmly closed when he saw a building with the words 'Spirit of Liberty' fixed to its walls. Not fully understanding the meaning, he hurriedly drew a picture in his Bible and made a note of the words he'd seen.

Not long after, Daphne's dad announced, 'We've decided to move back to India and set up home there.'

'Why? I thought you were settled here. Why go back now?'

'We were unsure as to what to do, but when holidaying there, your mum woke up one morning and said, "Let's build a house in India." What could I say? I feel it is right to take her home. You and the others are doing well.'

Daphne was devastated. She felt bereft at not being able to see them as often as she would like. India was not just around the corner, but 5 000 miles away.

'I'll miss you, but you must do what is best. I'll not stand in your way. How do you feel about it, Mum?'

'I'd like to go home. I think the time is right. We have land over there. We want to build a house so you and the family can visit.'

Daphne held back her tears.

Hugging her parents she said, 'If that is what you want, then you have my blessing.'

Visiting India to oversee the foundations of their new home, things hadn't worked out as they'd wished. Refused planning permission, they had to find an alternative site. The foundations laid, they returned to England to await the completion of their house in Odisha.

Relaxing in front of a warm fire, with Ivan and Daphne, Mr and Mrs Soraine showed the photos of the new building.

'Here's one I took from the lighthouse, looking down on the foundations.'

Ivan was drawn to a flagpole in the background.

'That flag.'

'What about it?'

'It has three horizontal stripes, green, white and saffron. It's similar to the Italian one but our colours lie vertically.'

'That's right. It's the Indian flag. It may well have similar colours, but the Italian flag does not have a wheel.'

Ivan was intrigued at the mention of a wheel. 'What do you mean?'

Mr Soraine showed him a picture of India's national flag. Ivan's stomach churned. He'd seen the wheel before. A surge of energy bubbled up as the full realisation of his mysterious dream washed over him. The wheel he had seen in his dream was there before his eyes, imprinted on the national flag of India.

'In the year I was born, 1921,' said Mr Soraine, 'Mohandas Gandhi, known as Mahatma, meaning Great Soul, proposed a flag design to the Indian National Congress. Originally it had two colours - red for the Hindus, and green for the Muslims. In the centre was a traditional spinning wheel, symbolizing Indian self-reliance. The flag was modified to include a white stripe in the centre for other religious communities. Later, to avoid sectarian associations with the colour scheme, saffron, white and green were chosen for the three bands. These represent courage and sacrifice, peace and truth, faith and chivalry respectively.

'Prior to India's independence on 15th August 1947, it was agreed that the flag must be acceptable to everyone. The colours remained the same, but the spinning wheel was replaced by the Ashoka Chakra, representing the eternal wheel of law.'

'Ashoka Chakra? What do you mean?'

'Ashoka was an emperor who lived around 304 BC to 232 BC. His rule stretched from the Hindu Kush to the Bay of Bengal. It was India's first great empire. Ashoka raised the quality of social justice, and after his conquest of Kalinga, he was remorseful and embraced Buddhism. Reverence for life, tolerance, compassion and peaceful co-existence became the cornerstones of his administration.

'It's said that he outlawed slavery and capital punishment, and then introduced environmental regulations. When younger, I learnt that Chakra was associated with tantric and yogic traditions of Hinduism and Buddhism. Chakra is a Sanskrit word meaning *spinning wheel of energy.*'

A few weeks later, Ivan and Daphne were browsing in a bookshop. Facing away from each other, Daphne picked up a book entitled, [2] They're Killing an Innocent Man.

Suddenly she sensed a burden for India heavily on her heart. Such was her concern she turned to Ivan. He looked her way. His eyes were awash with tears, for in his hand, he held a book about India.

Spontaneously, each said, 'I think God is telling us something.'

---

2 *They're Killing an Innocent Man by John Gilman.*

A Billion ...and Forty

The family reunion in their new home with Ivan and Daphne was a joyous occasion for Mr and Mrs Soraine. Settling well in India, the visitors were looking forward to three weeks' respite.

'I'm keen to tell others about Jesus, Mr Soraine,' announced Ivan.

'Be careful! You can get yourself into a lot of trouble here for mentioning Jesus as freely as you do.'

Mr Soraine sat back in his chair.

'India is a big place. It has over a billion people. That's more than the entire population of Australia and New Zealand combined, and larger than the total population of Europe.'

'Wow!'

Mr Soraine sensed Ivan's naivety of such a vast country and thought it right to enlighten him before he got himself thrown out.

'I read somewhere that of the billion, there are only twenty-five million Christians. The major religions are Hinduism, Islam, Sikhism, Buddhism, Jainism, Zoroastrianism, Judaism and the Baha'i faith. About 84% of the population is Hindu. Islam forms about 12%, but that number is growing fast.'

A billion or just one, it didn't matter to Ivan. Everyone was a soul to share the Good News of Jesus. The gentle warning and insight had not fallen on closed ears.

'Who can I speak with about Jesus?'

'I'll take you and Daphne to meet Matthew.'

On their way, Ivan saw unkempt children stealing food from a shrine to a Hindu god. A woman in a sari sat nearby. As they passed she covered her face and scurried away.

'Did you see that?'

'See what?'

'Those children stealing food, and that woman running away.'

'You'll get used to that. The kids are orphans. They scavenge for food and steal whatever they can. Was the woman wearing a white sari with no jewellery?'

'Dirty white, I would say. She looked frightened.'

'She'll have been fearful of putting a bad omen on you. She'll be a widow.'

'What do you mean?'

'Some believe that if a widow's shadow falls on them it brings bad luck.'

The three weaved their way through the stifling back streets, arriving at the local Baptist Church. 'I'll leave you to find your own way back.'

'Can I help you?' asked a man in his late thirties.

'Ivan Squillino. This is my wife, Daphne. We're looking for a man named Matthew.'

The man beamed. 'That's me. I'm the pastor here.' They shook hands. 'I sense you're both born again and longing to tell others of Jesus.'

The visitors smiled. From that moment, God sealed their friendship. 'I've been praying three years for this day. God brought you here. You've come to see the children.'

Ivan and Daphne looked surprised.

'I have a resource centre not far from here. I'll take you to see it.'

Coming to a small building no larger than a double garage, their hearts sank.

'This is it. It's home for 40 children.'

The two could not believe their eyes. Of mud construction, it had a rice stalk covered roof, which resembled thatching. Its walls were crumbling. Inside the ramshackled building, blackness hit them as if struck by blindness. Adjusting their vision from the bright Indian day to the confinement of the building, their eyes fell on a host of shabbily dressed children of all ages, sizes and ethnic origin. Nothing had prepared them for the wide brown eyes of the children fixing on them.

A little boy of three years or younger sat mesmerised on the stone floor staring at Daphne. Catching his infectious smile, compassion overwhelmed her. Almost in tears, she could hardly regain her composure.

Although she had seen many poor children in Africa, this colliding of eyes had somehow conveyed more than words could utter. While Matthew told Ivan of his frustrations, hopes and dreams, Daphne absorbed all that she saw and felt.

'Sorry I can't offer you refreshment. What little I have is for the children. I'm glad salvation is free and abundant! I'm grateful God has provided this place. Life is hard for them without parents. I see to their needs as best as I can. I tell them about Jesus and teach them to read and write. There's no hope for them in this country if they remain illiterate. They eat, sleep and learn here.'

Ivan glanced around the tiny room.

'Forty children sleep here?'

Matthew pointed to the floor.

'It's here or on the streets. They're abandoned orphans. I can only dream of what you have back home.'

His thoughts distant, a tear fell to Matthew's cheek. A vision not shared or talked about at that time filled his thoughts.

'I sense God has started to answer my prayer. He's sent you two.'

Seeing the harsh environment in which Matthew worked, he longed to say, *Sketch what you want and I'll provide it.* Without doubt, Ivan knew that God had prepared his heart and directed his path to meet Matthew, long before stepping onto India's soil. Yet he hesitated.

Four Small Words

His hesitancy lingered.

The Lord gave Daphne compelling words.

'We must help them. Draw up a list of the things you need.'

Ivan shuddered at the enormity of the task. It would take a giant leap of faith if they were to achieve success. Ivan longed for reassurance that it was what God wanted them to do.

Confirmation came when Matthew sketched the building which God had shown him.

Ivan had seen the same image in his dream. The one he'd drawn in his Bible and written in the margin –

Spirit of Liberty

Ivan and Daphne knew that God was directing them to service in India. They felt at peace when assurance came through God's Word.

And we know that for those who love God all things work together for good, for those who are called according to his purpose (Romans 8:28).

The vision confirmed, Ivan asked Matthew about the widow.

'I don't know her. Had the practice of Sati remained legal, I doubt if India would have any widows.'

The guests looked puzzled.

'The practice of Sati - also known as Suttee - is a funeral ritual among some Hindu communities. A recently widowed woman either volunteers or is forced to die on her husband's funeral pyre. Although banned in India since 1829, the practice continues in some remote areas.

'If the husband dies, his wife has a choice; marry her husband's brother or live the widow's life. Their families often ostracise the widow, sexually abuse her or sell her into slavery. Society shuns these Hindu widows. They become the poorest of the poor. Their families see them as a financial drain. They cannot remarry or wear jewellery. Forced to shave their heads, they wear white. Even their shadow is considered to bring calamity. Those widows who refuse to die in ritual Sati endure daily humiliation. They beg for alms, live completely apart from society and endure extreme poverty.'

Ivan sensed a deep burden for the widows' plight.

'It seems so hostile from the love we have in Jesus. Is there anyone to help you?'

'There's Solomon. He's not here at the moment. He's in Hyderabad. I'll send for him. He's a good lad.'

Ivan saw in his eyes the love he had for his charges and questioned whether he himself could do what Matthew was doing. Again, he scanned the shack and pictured the schools back home with all their facilities and resources.

When they shared with their local church, what they had seen and how God had directed them to that place, the church members had no hesitation to pray, but a miracle was needed in terms of financial support.

Reflection

Assured that the children in India were firmly in God's plan, Ivan and Daphne told everyone they met of their plight.

Such was their zeal that they, along with others, undertook all manner of fundraising events to raise the desperately needed cash.

Within six months, God had provided the money for the building project to begin.

Pastor Matthew's congregation of around 60 people were mainly fisher folk with their children.

Devoted to caring for those around him, life was hard. Poverty was not far from his eyes, especially in those struggling to survive by scavenging. With no means of his own, he'd prayed relentlessly that God would answer his prayers and those of the children.

Here's an example of their prayers.

Dear Jesus, Thank you for your love and provision for us. We ask that you keep Pastor Matthew and Solomon safe. For those who do not know you, we ask that they too will understand how much you love them and pray that they will one day give their hearts to you. Lord, look after us. You see how poor we are and thank you that we don't worship idols or things that are dead. Please help us, as we want a good place to sleep and to learn. Bring your kingdom in our place. Thank you for loving us. Amen.

Solomon, a sibling of one sister and three brothers, was the son of a fishing father he never knew. He was a year old when his mother, following the tragic death of his father, struggled to bring up the family. She was a twenty-two year old widow with no income or prospects of ever marrying again.

A Christian family, they had no worldly possessions and lived in abject poverty. Solomon's mother took whatever work she could to support her children.

Twelve thousand miles away, people in America hearing of her plight had sent money to support her and the children. For some unknown reason, the full amount never reached them. The misappropriation of the funds became known when the donors visited India. The reaction was swift, final and heart-rending. The monetary gift ceased, leaving the struggling widow to raise her family without financial assistance.

Solomon was ten years old when 28 year-old Pastor Matthew took him under his wing. He grew up to be a well-spoken, well-educated, fine young man who helped his surrogate father whenever he could.

Two years prior to Ivan and Daphne's visit to India, Solomon was at the resource centre telling the children about Jesus when a young Hindu girl of almost 13 years of age, timidly peeped into the hut. He looked her way, paused and beckoned her to enter. From that day, she often visited to listen to what he had to say. He sensed she was no ordinary girl. Her long black hair, brown eyes, smooth face, warm smile and gentle manner when engaging with the children, captured his attention.

Many other children had visited and then sneaked away never to return, but this one remained. In the ensuing weeks, their eyes met one day. Instantly he knew without doubt that she was the one for him.

Even in western society such a relationship would meet with disapproval.

This was a close-knit community. He worshipped one God, she many. He was the teacher, she an inquisitive intruder. Penniless, and caring for 40 dependent destitute children, he had no means of offering her security.

The community, steeped in convention, custom and tradition capable of arousing village passions of an unwanted nature, he knew if he spoke to her, she would be ostracised. Hiding his feelings from her, he buried them deep enough so as not to hinder his work. No matter how hard he tried to conceal or deny love, in its moment of celebration, love would not be silenced. Suppress it he did to his satisfaction. Holding back from uttering her name or showing the slightest affection towards her, he held loving words in his head while locking his longings firmly in his heart.

As for the beautiful girl named Seeta, the youngest of five children and named after a Hindu goddess, she'd seen how hard the teacher boy worked. So near, yet worlds apart, she knew such innocent love was forbidden on fear of death. She'd seen his eyes cry out that which was in his heart and hoped that he too had seen her longings.

The months slipped by as Solomon and Seeta held in their hearts how they felt for one another. Both knew that to touch, speak or exchange the slightest physical gesture would dishonour her family and bring trouble to them both. Simply put, Solomon and Seeta did not stand a chance of developing a loving relationship.

A Date to Remember

India's Independence Day celebration, 15th August 1997, at 6 p.m., is a date that Solomon locked in his heart. Walking down the village's main street, he set eyes on Seeta. With chest tightening and heart pounding, he wanted to say so much to her. Unable to verbalise what was in his heart from shaking with fear, he stood silently gazing at her. A gentle smile set his face alight. Aware that time would be limited before others saw him, his hesitancy was broken.

'I love you and want to marry you.'

Breaking all convention, he had given her a rare glimpse of the content of his heart, hoping and longing that the love he had for her would be reciprocated.

Leaning against a wall, she fixed her eyes upon him. Her silent scream, *Yes! Yes!* bubbling within her failed to make the airwaves. Yet somehow, Solomon grasped her reply.

Suppressing their desire to touch, she asked, 'When shall we marry?'

'In five years' time.'

She now 13, and he 18, Solomon considered it would give him sufficient time to find a good job and earn enough money to support her.

'Two years,' bartered Seeta. 'I broke all the rules for you. I love you.'

'Four,' he said.

'Three,' she replied.

He shook his head. 'I must make something of my life before I can marry you. I've given you my promise. Give me four years and then I'll marry you.'

Parting company, each held a glimmer of hope simmering in their hearts.

Within six months of Solomon's promise of marriage to Seeta, rumours of their clandestine love circulated around the village. When challenged by her parents, Seeta confessed that she loved Solomon and that they had agreed to marry.

Her dad was furious.

'You're a Hindu. I'll not allow it. I forbid you to go anywhere near that shambles of a resource centre. Do you understand?'

'We agreed to marry in four years' time. I'll then be seventeen,' she pleaded.

'Four years or one, you'll not marry him. You are to marry a fine Hindu boy.'

Tears swept down Seeta's cheeks at the thought of marrying someone she didn't love. On a number of occasions, she'd sneaked out to see Solomon, but her parents dragged her home and locked her away for many days.

'We've arranged for you to marry a very nice Hindu boy,' smiled Seeta's mother.

'But I don't want to marry anyone except the teacher.'

'You'll marry who I say. It's your father's wish. I've told your sisters to help you put on the Salwar Kameez.'
[A long ceremonial tunic worn along with baggy trousers indicating the girl is engaged].

'I'll not wear it! If I cannot marry the teacher, I'll not marry anyone!'

'Teacher! Teacher!' screamed her mother. 'What do you want with him? He's bad - no good, no job, no prospects, no life. Who will feed your children? We won't. We can barely feed ourselves. He's not one of us. No good will come of it. I've told you, he's a no-good, bad man.'

Tears drenched her cheeks as she slumped on a chair. Sobbing bitterly, Seeta was adamant.

'I love the teacher. He's the one I'll marry.'

Seeing their daughter's determination, Seeta's parents locked her away for 20 long days, hoping to starve her into submission.

Enduring her brothers' and sisters' taunts, she cried constantly. She sent messages to Solomon via the orphans, pleading for him to come and save her. Longing for him to take her away, he never came. Seeta felt abandoned.

Strict religious ordinances and Hindu convention, along with the unspoken power of collective village opinion, prevented Solomon from going anywhere near her house. The heartache of not seeing her at the orphanage and his inability to pose questions caused him deep distress.

The family meeting with Seeta's prospective husband did not go well. She was adamant she would marry the teacher and refused further offers of marriage. Her punishment was long lonely hours of separation and silence, locked away in her room.

Seeta's relatives viewed their actions as those of loving parents trying to teach their child the error of her way.

Honour and centuries of custom and practice ingrained in the herd instinct of village life and the expectation of others and their longing for acceptance in society was the norm.

Solomon was also under pressure. The first conflict came unexpectedly through his mother.

'Why do you work so hard with those children? They are nothing to you. Let some other do the work. You should find some positive work to do - like other boys - and look after me. You'll not live on love. How do you expect to support a wife and family if you have no income? Matthew pays you nothing.'

She had only Solomon's interest at heart.

Succumbing to the pressure, he left home to look for work in Hyderabad.

Clinging to the Bible events she had heard Solomon tell the children, Seeta longed for them to be true. One Creator God, one Saviour, one Redeemer, one love? It all seemed so far from reality as she cried the long hours away, alone.

The gossip that Solomon had left home cruelly plagued her mind.

Where is he?
Has he abandoned me?

Opposition

Excited at the prospects of a new building, Matthew was overjoyed when Solomon returned home.

Ivan and Daphne had worked hard to raise the money needed to support the children. The land bought and the foundations dug, Matthew relinquished his position as local Baptist Church pastor to focus his energy on the new project.

The walls of the orphanage were a metre high when Ivan arrived to view the progress. Excitement lingered over the new construction as the children thanked Jesus for their new home and answered prayers. Soon the roof would be on and the children admitted.

Following a good night's sleep, Matthew and Ivan rose early to inspect the site. Approaching the building, their hearts sank.

'Oh no!' cried Matthew. 'Who could have done such a wicked act?'

'Men came in the night and broke down the walls,' a labourer told them.

'What men?'

'I don't know.'

Not only had the vandals smashed down the walls, they'd sledgehammered the foundations. Devastated at such wanton destruction, they prayed intently.

Rising to his feet, Ivan sensed the hopelessness of the situation. The pain at seeing a dream destroyed hit him as hard as any physical blow. The cost of the rebuilding would take every penny they'd raised. There would not be enough money to complete the project.

Physically and emotionally drained, they contemplated what action to take. Unable to do any more, Ivan trusted Jesus to sort out the problem and left for home.

Back in England, he made a profound decision of faith that would affect the lives of many lost souls. He phoned Matthew.

'Abandon building.'

This was not what Matthew wanted to hear. The phone fell silent. The years of struggle, prayers and dreams crowded in on him. Holding his breath, he prayed hard. The long pause lengthened. Ivan broke the silence.

'Look for land somewhere else.'

Prayers answered, Matthew rejoiced, glorifying His Saviour. 'What about the finance?'

Another prolonged silence.

The Apostle Paul's words of encouragement echoed loudly in Ivan's ears.

He who began a good work in you will carry it on to completion until the day of Christ Jesus (Philippians 1:6).

'The Lord will provide,' assured Ivan.

As in previous times, Scripture brought courage and strength.

That is what the word of God does, commented Ivan.

Within seven weeks, Matthew had found alternative land and God had supplied the money to buy not only the land but also the adjoining land surrounding the proposed orphanage. The foundations dug and the walls built, £700 was needed to roof the building. Funds were desperately low and costs were spiralling.

Matthew feared a roofless building exposed to the approaching monsoon rain would destroy all the hard work. Ivan was down to his last few pounds when forwarding the money to pay outstanding bills.

When the money arrived in India, the exchange rate shown in rupees had had an additional £700 added to the cash. God had provided exactly the right amount.

A monetary crisis in Europe had necessitated a readjustment to the value of the euro. Some may say that was a fluke or a chance occurrence. Ivan and Matthew knew otherwise and thanked God for His provision.

The furnishings in place and the electricity, water and sanitation installed, the Spirit of Liberty Children's Home was established.

With faith-challenging ongoing costs, Ivan and Daphne depended totally on God to supply the monthly financial outlay required.

Working hard at the orphanage, Solomon hadn't seen Seeta. He still loved her, but couldn't approach the house or her for fear of inviting trouble.

Seeta's love for Solomon had not grown cold. Somewhere deep in her heart she kept hope alive.

Her older sisters had come and dragged her into the sleeping area, stripped her of her sari and forced her into the ceremonial garb of a promised woman.

Trying to resist, she yielded to their cumulative strength. Satisfied that she was ready to meet her prospective husband, they left her crying on the bed, heartbroken.

A little later, the family frogmarched her to a house. Friendly chatter ensued between her father and hosts as they negotiated the union of the two families. The prospective husband sat silently looking on.

Seeta dared not look his way, adamantly repeating in her head, *I'll not marry him. I'm going to marry the teacher. He promised me.*

The arrangements made, the family returned home, pleased that their daughter would soon be married.

'I'll not marry him,' she said on arriving home. A rowdy argument followed. Suddenly, her sisters hauled her into the bedroom, and ripped off the ceremonial dress, leaving Seeta almost naked. Her pillow was no stranger to her tears as she lay disconsolately crying her eyes out. Internalising her screams of, *I love you! I love you!* she held on to a thin thread of hope that one day Solomon would take her to be his wife. Her fear erupted like a volcano. She doubted her ability to sustain months of persistent family badgering to marry some other. The weeks passed and the pressure for her to marry abated.

Everything was working out fine at the orphanage until Solomon's mother again expressed concern.

'You're working too hard, Solomon. I tell you, go and get a proper job.'

The bombardment came from two sides. Matthew feared what might happen if he left.

'I nurtured you to take over from me. Please, Solomon. I beg you not to leave.'

His pleadings fell on stony ground.

'I have to go, Pastor. I work here day and night without pay or complaining. I want a normal life. I need to help my mother, get a place of my own, and be able to support a wife and family. I'll have none of these things if I don't find a job. You're a bachelor. That life is not for me.'

Conflict raged in Solomon's heart. He was torn between caring for the children, and earning good money in hope of marrying Seeta. Like a tug of war, the game only ceased when he ran away to Hyderabad.

Solomon's mother was relieved, but Pastor Matthew couldn't share her joy. He struggled to maintain the taxing pace of the children's daily routine. Praying and fasting, he asked God to ease his workload and show him the way forward.

Manipulation

Further gruelling months passed for Seeta without word of Solomon. Her mother knew of his whereabouts.

'It's a good time to get Seeta married to some eligible Hindu boy.'

Seeta was devastated but the pressure to obey her mother was intense.

'If you refuse to marry the man we have chosen for you and insist on marrying that Christian, you not only dishonour yourself, but also your parents. You'll shame us and we'll be ostracised by the community. We'll be disgraced. We will be outcasts in our own village. Death will be our release. For the sake of family honour, we will have no option but to die.'

'You can't. I won't let you do such a thing.'

'Then do as we say and marry the Hindu boy. If you refuse, your father and I will poison ourselves. We cannot have our honour tarnished.'

Her parents seriously intended to carry out the threat.

How can I be happy, knowing I am the cause of their death?

After many hours of reasoning and agonising, she decided to obey and live with the consequences.

This would be no marriage of love. The small dowry offered to the potential husband would fall into insignificance at Seeta's profound heartache. Self-sacrifice, cruel endurance, deep unhappiness and a lifetime of tormenting thoughts of what might have been had she married the teacher boy, was to be her lot. Her tear-drenched pillow was the prelude to agony.

All seemed lost. Hope had died and fear took root.

Solomon knew nothing of Seeta's forced marriage until after the event. The girl who had captured his heart was gone; lost to some other, never to return. Broken-hearted, he wept and longed for news of an error. There was no mistake.

Two young, inexperienced people of Indian origin, constrained by cultural convention, stood on opposite sides of a wide chasm. But God's eyes were on Solomon and Seeta.

Within days of the forced child-wedding, Seeta walked away from the marriage. Unable to endure her new life, she ran to her sister's house. Seeing Seeta's distress, compassion stirred her sister, as loving arms enfolded the vulnerable fourteen-year old.

The sister confronted Seeta's husband and his family saying the marriage, such as it was, was at an end and that Seeta wanted none of the forced relationship.

The Unexpected

Meanwhile in England, Ivan had a dream about Germany. While sleeping, he saw himself step from a train in Rosenheim being welcomed by two people he knew. Weeks later, he realised the significance of the dream when he received an invitation to preach. On his first visit to Germany, Ivan sensed God calling him to minister there. God had already planted similar thoughts in Daphne's heart. Spending a year in Germany seemed impossible. Trusting God implicitly, they knew that if He wanted them there He would find a way for them to go.

Asking the Lord for direction, the answer came swiftly. Beyond Daphne's wildest expectations, her boss held her job open for a year. Believing this was confirmation, they left for Germany, trusting that God would provide a place to live and the means of support. God had already prepared a German couple to provide financial support and a place to live.

Ivan and Daphne's transport needs proved to be a surprise to some - to others, perfectly orchestrated by a loving Saviour.

Knowing he would be in Germany for twelve months, he felt it would be safer if he bought a vehicle with left hand drive.

Four weeks prior to leaving for Germany, his desire to sell his own car and buy a left-handed vehicle seemed unattainable. Trusting Jesus, he felt compelled to buy a periodical which advertised second hand cars. On removing the magazine from the shelf, his eyes immediately fixed on a left hand drive Mercedes 190 E. Scanning the pages, he realised that this car was the only left-handed drive advertised. The vendor had just returned from Germany and needed a right-handed drive!

Contact made, following inspection and test drive, an exchange of cars was agreed.

Ivan and Daphne were set to drive across the continent.

Truly God-sent, the Mercedes provided excellent service throughout their year's stay, passing the stringent German roadworthiness test.

Called to a variety of locations spanning countries and continents, Ivan remained constant in prayer. His animated preaching and natural ability to engage those he meets, his stability in the love of the Lord and his steadfast dedication to Bible truths continue to inspire him to seek a close relationship with Jesus.

His early morning mountain prayer walks in Bavaria preceded every platform engagement. Keen to know the *'mind of Christ'* (1 Corinthians 2:16) he would fast and pray prior to healing meetings or times of ministry.

Ivan views every human experience as a learning situation and an opportunity to share the gospel. Fascinated by the intricate workmanship built into antique timepieces, he was thrilled when a friend showed him his watch. Imprinted on the watch face were the words, *Watch and Pray*. A novel setting for apt words which reflect the deeper characteristic of both as men of prayer.

There are too many events to relate where God revealed His power. Although all are worthy of telling, one is particularly worthy of note. The occurrence happened at an evening meeting, when his subject was the abundance of God's grace. As was his practise, Ivan looked for a private place to kneel in prayer and commune with God. This was something he'd done from the outset of his Christian walk. By 'dwelling in the secret place', he'd experienced the assurance of Psalm 91.

On his knees in union with His Maker, God told him that five people would open their hearts to the gospel message and invite Jesus into their lives.

God revealed to him that a woman would commit suicide that night if she did not hear a word from God.

That evening, unbeknown to him, a woman entered the meeting and sat in desperate anguish. Hoping, longing that God would give her some word that would ease her sorrow, she sat alone near the back of the hall. The woman believed that the peoples of the world had forgotten her. Clinging to a glimmer of hope that the Creator God would let her know that He loved her, she waited for the service to begin.

Ivan knew that if he failed God that night, then for one lone woman, hope would be lost, along with a valuable soul.

Sharing the Good News of Jesus' love to a congregation of hundreds, he obeyed God and directed his words to an unknown woman seated somewhere in the congregation.

There, in a packed church, Ivan paused and then lovingly said, 'I am here to tell you, you have a future.' He then continued to proclaim Jesus as his Lord and King.

That evening, four people opened their hearts to Jesus.

After the meeting, a woman approached him. 'Tonight I would have killed myself, had you not said I have a future. I want to know Jesus.' She then asked Jesus into her life.

Back in India, Matthew was struggling on without Solomon. He told no one of the pain he suffered. Matthew was ill. Summer was ending when his illness reached a critical stage. Unable to continue working at the orphanage, a hospital bed became his home. Overtaken by a terminal illness, his suffering was short-lived as cancer took the orphans' sole carer. He was 42 years old.

When the church elders buried the body in the grounds of the orphanage, there was much sadness and anxiety amongst the orphans as they mourned the loss of their father figure.

Guilt and Sorrow

Solomon was earning good money in Hyderabad when his mother sent word of Pastor Matthew's death. Rushing home, tired, distraught and fatigued from the journey, he ran to Matthew's grave. Incapable of rational thought, he fell on his knees, clawing at the earth in desperation to reach Matthew's body. He so longed to hold him in his arms and ask for forgiveness for abandoning him. Solomon's agonising cries brought the children running to the grave.

'Come,' said the older boys trying to stop him scooping the soil with his bare hands. Surrounded by loving arms, he eventually stopped sobbing, as the words, 'Don't leave us,' filled his ears.

Dragging himself away from the children, he rushed to the Soraine's house.

'Pray for me. Pray for me,' he cried with tears streaming down his cheeks.

Mr Soraine, now well into his seventies, still possessed a charisma and a voice that made people listen. He, however, was not the one to speak. While compassion overwhelmed him, his wife spoke words of comfort and assurance. Amidst her tears, she prayed, and then said lovingly, 'You must not worry. Things will work out well. You look after the children and we'll look after you.'

Her words and the kindly act of caring for him given at such a critical time were rooted in his heart. The loving couple, who had met Jesus towards the closing of their lives, were where Jesus wanted them to be at that vital hour in Solomon's life.

He was no stranger to hardship or despair. Battling with guilt, he returned to the orphanage, feeling much stronger than when last he had been there.

Solomon phoned Ivan in Germany.

'It's Pastor Matthew, Papa. He's dead.'

Ivan froze. Knowing he must remain strong with no hint of fear or worry in his voice, he took courage in knowing that Jesus' love would flow.

'Dead! How?'

'I don't know all the details. He died in hospital. He must have known he was ill long before I left him. I can't understand it. He showed no symptoms and never once complained. His family say it was cancer.'

Ivan wanted to comfort Solomon with loving arms. Softly, words slipped from his tongue.

'Well, he's with the Lord now. Are the children safe?'

'They are, but they cry a lot. They took his death badly. It was such a shock. They know Pastor Matthew is with the Lord. I don't know what to do.'

Daphne saw the anguish in Ivan's face. Seeing his expression, she took the phone.

'You have to be strong for the children's sake, Solomon. You'll have to look after things there until we can see you. You're capable. Above all else, look after the children well. You know what to do.'

Ivan composed himself.

'You are to take over things, just as Joshua did when Moses died. It was Pastor Matthew's wish. Remember, God is with you and sees everything you do. Trust Him.'

Solomon agreed to take on Matthew's role with Ivan's guidance.

Mr and Mrs Soraine needed no persuasion in supporting Solomon and became pillars of strength for their charge.

The daily running of the orphanage was a daunting task for the young lad but he knew he could depend on Daphne's parents. At that time, Solomon had not totally committed himself to Jesus.

Mr Soraine taught him English grammar and the spoken word for which Solomon was graciously thankful. He was soon speaking the language fluently.

In some small way, Matthew had been a Moses to the children. With unyielding faith, he'd gathered them under his wing. He had seen the land God had promised him - a sanctuary for the unloved. He had obeyed God's call, providing food, shelter and the gospel. He'd given them hope and believed that Jesus would answer prayer. Faithful to God's call, Matthew, like Moses, was not to see the outcome of his pleadings with a loving God.

Ivan had aptly named Solomon, Joshua, for when Moses died, God commanded Joshua to be 'strong and courageous' and not to be 'discouraged' and that He would be with him wherever he went (Joshua 1:9).

Solomon harboured much guilt for leaving Matthew. Distraught at the loss of his mentor, he fasted many days. He so wanted to shed the remorse, trust Jesus and walk in the way God would lead him. It was decision time. After much heart-searching, he committed his life totally to Jesus. God had plans for Ivan's *Joshua*.

Now 22 years old, he worked hard and prayed constantly. One night while sleeping, he heard words so clearly spoken. *Now be strong and don't run away. Neither be afraid. I'll always be with you.*

Opening the Way

When in Germany, Ivan and Daphne had felt God wanted them to work permanently in that country. He had other plans. Moving back to England and preparing to sell their house, a fellowship in Glasgow, Scotland, invited Ivan and Daphne to a conference.

Now almost 60, Ivan had lived by faith. Aware of their situation, God opened the way for them to attend by directing the fellowship in Glasgow to pay for all the costs.

After the conference the pastor and a number of church leaders invited Ivan to join them permanently in Glasgow as an evangelist.

Trusting Jesus to guide them in making the right decision, Ivan and Daphne prayed earnestly that God would confirm their calling. There were many concerns prayerfully to consider. The large family in India was constantly on their minds and in their prayers.

Confirmation came quickly. On their return from Glasgow, a friend offered to buy their house. The man knew nothing of the pending move.

No longer requiring a car with left hand steering, Ivan sensed the need to exchange or sell the Merc.

Thinking no more of the matter, he drove off to a dental appointment. With his mouth agape and instruments tapping his teeth, conversation was difficult.

'I need to see you in a week's time,' said the dentist. Glancing from his window he asked, 'Is that your car?'

'Yes! It's for sale.'

More than interested, after looking over the car he announced, 'I'll buy it.'

A cash sale, Ivan thanked Jesus for his enduring love.

On Ivan's return, the dentist commented, 'I have no idea why I bought your car.'

Ivan knew.

The fellowship in Glasgow welcomed the orphanage into its care. While the responsibility of overseeing the daily activities and welfare of the children and workers in India remained fully the responsibility of Ivan and Daphne, the burden of fundraising was eased a little through various events. The wide spectrum of churches planted by the fellowship became open to tell of God's work in India.

Given a free hand to evangelise, Ivan trudged the streets going from door to door, telling everyone about Jesus' love.

Trouble and Trauma

Solomon was organising the breakfast when a distraught youth barged into the orphanage.

'Come quickly, Solomon! There's a riotous fellow going crazy and frightening the children!'

'Out! Out! Out of my house!' screamed a drunken vagrant, shooing fearful helpers and children out of the building.

'What are you doing? Stop terrifying the children!' yelled Solomon, gathering the little ones around him.

The man yanked an official looking document from his pocket. Glaring at Solomon, he waved the papers furiously in the air screaming, 'I want you out - every last one of you! Out! Do you hear? Out of my property!'

Solomon snatched the document from the intruder as more distressed children appeared. His heart sank when reading the document. The buildings and grounds no longer belonged to those who had laboured so hard to support their work. The man was Matthew's brother. He now owned the orphanage.

With a sneaky grin, his bulbous, bloodshot eyes projected evil.

'Out! You have no right to be here. The property belongs to me.'

Solomon tried to calm the crying children.

'We have nowhere to go,' he pleaded.

'That's not my problem.'

There were many tears and broken hearts that day as the children, widows and helpers were ushered by the vagrant out of the building and into the street.

With utter lack of empathy, he secured the door with a large lock. Turning, toward the destitute orphans, widows and helpers, he yelled in delight, 'Away with you all! Be gone I say!'

Sobbing in anguish, there in the street, the children huddled together in need of comfort. With nowhere to go, Solomon turned to Daphne's dad.

Deeply perturbed, he arrived at Mr Soraine's house. 'Matthew's brother has thrown everyone out of the orphanage. He has placed a huge lock on the door. He says the building belongs to him.'

Confident and bold, Mr Soraine said calmly, 'Does he now? We'll see about that! Follow me.'

A man not to be dealt with lightly, he was soon banging on the door of the newly-installed resident.

'Go away!' yelled the incumbent.

A strong man, Mr Soraine broke the lock and entered the building. Little is known of the conversation between the two. Matthew's brother abandoned the place quicker than he had entered.

There was great relief, much prayer and excitement when the children moved back into their home. The terrifying few hours of uncertainty and distress at an end, the orphanage soon returned to its normal activities.

A few days after Matthew's brother had thrown the children out of the orphanage, he died of some mysterious illness.

More trouble was brewing.

Hope Challenged

Things were quiet at the orphanage as everyone went about their duties, feeling more secure. During this period, Solomon had not seen or heard of Seeta. The village gossips had been quick to say he'd run away again. Indeed, he had left the village, but had not run away.

Feeling totally abandoned, Seeta slipped into a troubled mindset. As a year slipped by with no news of Solomon, her depressive state hit depths of despair and hopelessness.

Alone on her bed, her whole life crossed before her as every minor incident magnified into major proportions. Her head reeling in pain. Solomon's Bible stories were far from her thoughts. The hopelessness of her life hit hard. The sweet memories of Solomon were fast dissipating as if they had never happened.

Drained of all hope and with no ease from her plight, in a dreamlike state she stood on her bed, flung her sari over a beam in the roof and secured it with a knot. With the dangling end, she made a loop and slipped it over her head pulling it taut around her neck. Balancing precariously on the edge of her bed, tears of desperation poured down her cheeks as she sought to end her life. Trembling with uncontrollable body shakes, she tried to suppress her vocal gasps. She closed her eyes, ready to die. In those desperate seconds, about to drop from off the bed, she heard a voice clearly speaking to her.

What's happened to your love? You live a righteous life. Don't doubt. You'll see the teacher. Don't doubt.

Surrounded by a sense of tremendous peace, she drew back. Throwing off the sari from around her neck, her tears of sorrow changed to tears of joy. She knew she was not alone. Seeta was 17 years old.

Not fully understanding what had happened to her, she knew beyond doubt that Solomon's God was real and alive. She could feel His Presence. Now with strength, her fear conquered and her life renewed, she knew that Jesus was with her. She trusted her Creator God that He would keep her safe and hold to His promise that one day she would see Solomon.

A year had passed since Seeta had met with Jesus. Her forced marriage far behind her, she held onto the hope that one day she would share her life with the teacher. She tried hard to cast out the crippling thoughts that he had forgotten his promise and had rejected her.

Meanwhile, there were great celebrations at the orphanage when Solomon returned home. He'd been studying hard. Having passed his Bible College exams, he was ready to step out further in faith.

Solomon had gone away a boy and returned a man. Ivan's *Joshua* was revealed in Pastor Solomon.

Caught Unawares

Solomon was surprised when Seeta's mother knocked boldly on his door.

'What are your intentions towards my daughter? She's done nothing but cry constantly ever since you left. You have a lot to account for, young man. She was in such a state she tried to kill herself.

'She says you made her a promise.'

Before Solomon could answer, the woman poured out her heart, confessing to the forced marriage.

'Stubborn girl. She'd be better without such as you. I've told her you're no good. This makes her cry even more. She even speaks to your God. I expect you'll marry some rich girl - now that you're educated and have a good job. You'll not prosper for abandoning my daughter.'

Solomon was lost for words. *Is it too much to ask or hope that Seeta has met with Jesus?* Without passion or sentiment for fear of seeming keen to marry the girl, he said, 'I gave her my word.'

He'd said enough. Off she ran to tell Seeta the outcome of the meeting.

Breaking all protocol Solomon ran to fulfil his promise to the sweet inquisitive girl who'd sneaked into the dilapidated shack so long ago.

Her family did not look upon him favourably when he entered their house. All that changed when he asked Seeta's father for her hand in marriage.

Seeta was hiding away when Solomon faced her dad.

'Come, Seeta,' urged her mother, 'You are to marry the teacher.'

For the first time, Seeta was nervous. When her mother ushered her into the room, all she saw was Solomon. Caught unawares, memories of their first meeting flashed before her eyes, followed by the sorrow, heartache and pain of uncertainty.

Can this really be happening to me?

She'd prayed for this day so many times. The cold agonising tears of despair vanished wetting her cheeks were tears of joy. The long years of separation, the many lonely hours of fear and crying, along with the torturous physiological ordeal of family and community rejection faded.

Solomon held back from expressing his love for fear of her parents' disapproval.

'I long to marry you,' he said.

Her smile conveyed consent.

Disquiet

News of Solomon's intention to marry Seeta spread throughout the village. A tight-knit community, diverse opinions erupted. Soon, many individuals with their own agendas stood at his door, persuading him to adopt their personal viewpoints. Faced with a conglomeration of concerns, Solomon was overwhelmed.

While the exact conversations are lost to speculative opinion, the visitors expressed forcefully two concerns, Seeta's marriage and Solomon, a Christian, marrying a Hindu.

Excluded from their deliberations was the fact that Seeta had met with Jesus, and the pressurised circumstances that had forced Seeta into a matrimonial arrangement she detested. As for her loving encounter with Jesus, she held it in her heart, longing to share her amazing spiritual experience with Solomon.

By giving his word to Seeta, some of his persuaders considered he'd compromised his call to the ministry. Solomon needed a miracle to make everything right. Fasting for days, and speaking to Jesus, he prayed constantly for assurance that he remained in God's will.

Daily on his knees at 4 a.m., he cried out.

'Lord, you see the situation. Please help me. You know my heart. I am wholly committed to you. You know how my family tried to stop me from going to Bible College. They said, "No good would come of it." You see how everyone is against me marrying Seeta. Even my own kin oppose me. What do you want, Lord? My work is with you. My life is yours.'

Seeta also felt the strain. Solomon's hesitance to fix a wedding date generated doubt. She cried incessantly, clinging to her fledgling faith that Jesus would somehow make things right.

Despite all the persuasive pressure, no matter how lovingly expressed by concerned individuals, he sensed deep within his heart that one day Seeta would be at his side, bringing lost souls into God's kingdom.

A further meeting of concerned individuals almost brought Solomon to tears. Knowing that God loved him, and that he was totally in His care, sincerity echoed loudly in his words.

'I love Jesus. That you know. I won't go against what he's planned for me. However, although I can't explain, I know that Seeta is the one to be at my side. What can I say?

'You see an impoverished Hindu girl - valueless, the lowest of the low in society, an outcast to be denigrated when passing by.

'Seeta is none of these. I see a soul for Jesus, a life to love, and an evangelist in the making.

'God gave a promise to Abraham and kept it. I, as a child of God, gave a promise to Seeta. Only my Heavenly Father can prevent the fulfilment of that promise.'

A prolonged silence prevailed until a well-respected elderly man who had listened intently but had said nothing, announced authoritatively to the surprise of his peers, 'You can marry her!'

The softening of the heart of the clearly respected man quashed dissenters and sanctioned their acceptance to abide by his decision.

Solomon did not need the permission of anyone of earthly stature. His loving Saviour had sorted things out. Thanking Jesus, he rushed to tell Seeta.

As children of God, Solomon and Seeta, born of love through Christ Jesus, their past forgiven and forgotten, were firmly in His care and called to His service.

Answered Prayer

Solomon's meeting with Seeta was brief. Her prayers answered, he'd come to claim her as his wife.

Now free to share the longings and aspirations of her heart, she said, 'I love Jesus. He spoke to me.'

Thank you Jesus, was his silent praise.

A lifetime to discover the heartaches and joys each had experienced, Solomon announced boldly, 'We'll marry at my church.'

'I'd like that,' she said, her softly-spoken voice vibrating in his ears.

'It was wrong of your father and I to force you into marriage,' confessed Seeta's mother after Solomon had gone. 'Can you ever forgive us? We should not have stopped you from seeing the pastor man.'

'You mean Solomon?'

'That's him. I am truly sorry.'

Seeta hugged her mother. 'I love you, Mum.'

When baptised, she went down under the water as Seeta, the name of a Hindu goddess, and rose as Sweta, meaning *as pure as milk*.

Not long after her water baptism, a wonderful event occurred. God blessed her by baptising her with His Spirit, praising God in a spiritual language.

Her fragile faith in Jesus prior to Him speaking to her had only been head knowledge. Now, holding Jesus firmly in her heart, He was forever in her thoughts, feelings and actions.

Giving thanks to a loving Saviour who had watched over them, Solomon and Sweta were married in the local church.

Singing, praising and prayer marked the happy occasion as the congregation including the children from the orphanage added their blessing to the union.

Sometime after the wedding, Sweta shared with Solomon the time Jesus had revealed himself to her. It was an emotional occasion. Both cried. They were thankful that Jesus was in the centre of their lives and praised God that they were able to share with others the good news of His love.

She had met Jesus, but others of her family had not. Filled with resolute determination to ensure that none of them was lost to idol worship, Sweta told her family about Jesus' love. She prayed that one day they would come to know Him.

Her prayers were answered when, within two months of Sweta's marriage to Solomon, her mother invited Jesus into her life. Six months later, there was further rejoicing in heaven and on earth when her father realised that Jesus was no fantasy. Soon, the whole family of sisters, brother, uncles, aunts and cousins invited Jesus into their lives.

Sweta was thrilled and wept tears of joy when her family passed through the waters of baptism - truly an answer to her prayers.

The church population expanded faster than it had for many years. Baptism by total immersion quickly followed and then, baptism in the Spirit.

Opposition

Ivan was at the orphanage when he was stirred by the suffering around him.

'The next time I'm here, we'll hold a healing mission.'

Solomon enthusiastically agreed.

'We'll erect a marquee in the orphanage grounds and invite the whole village.'

Solomon worked ceaselessly to ensure everything would run smoothly. The arrangements were complete when Ivan and Daphne arrived with two friends.

At least 40 families from surrounding villages gathered, keen to hear the gospel message and be healed. Excitement filled the air until Bajrang Dal, a Hindu militant group raised objections.

A Hindu Conference was scheduled for the very same day. Local Hindu leaders were determined to prevent the healing mission from taking place. They considered it an affront to their belief and set their minds to quash the event.

'If you attempt to hold a healing mission, you'll all be killed,' warned a prominent Hindu, clearly emphasising *all*.

This was no mean threat. There were many locals capable of carrying out the killings and would have had no qualms about burning and murdering infidels - as they believed followers of Jesus to be.

Should the healing mission go ahead or be postponed? The decision was taken out of Ivan's hands when the local police unexpectedly arrived.

'Where's this preacher fellow?' yelled a tall, broad shouldered police chief whose heavy handlebar moustache almost covered his cheeks.

'Where is he?'

The officer waved a leaflet containing Ivan's photo.

'I'm he,' said Ivan.

The officer motioned to his constables to seize him.

'What's the trouble?' asked a perplexed Ivan, as the police manhandled him. A large crowd gathered outside the orphanage. There were many concerned faces and anxious children.

'You are to come with us,' demanded the officer.

'It's alright,' said Ivan to those around him. 'Stay calm and don't worry. We'll be safe.'

The police officer escorted Ivan, Daphne and the two young helpers to the local police station. A crowd of believers followed, refusing to disperse. Outside the police station, they demanded their release.

Once inside the building, the police chief continued shouting and raging at Ivan. Taking papers from a filing cabinet, he banged them down hard on a table.

'You must sign this and then go.'

The papers contained acceptance that Ivan agreed to cancel the Healing Mission and return home.

He refused.

The man bellowed like an irate mafia boss exploding on hearing that his financial deal had gone wrong.

Money however, was not the issue. It was fear. Militants feared that love would rise up and peacefully overcome all opposition to its power.

Condemned without trial, the authorities were determined to ensure Ivan did not speak in public.

He - as did the police - knew that the India constitution had enshrined in law that all people are free to practise their religion without fear or hindrance.

Amid the officer's ranting, God revealed to Ivan that the man was in pain.

'I'd like a moment with you in private.'

Suddenly, the chief ceased his anger and directed Ivan to a back room.

'What is it?'

Filled with spiritual strength, he faced his aggressor. 'You don't frighten any of us. All we do is look after orphans. You're not fighting against us but against God.'

The officer stepped back, not knowing how to deal with such forceful words calmly delivered. A few moments of silence passed.

'I'm sorry. I'm only trying to do my job.'

'You have trouble with your back. You can't sleep at night for the pain.'

The officer looked surprised.

'How do you know? Who told you?'

Ivan smiled knowingly.

'May I pray for you?'

The man glared at him with suspicion. A more pregnant pause followed before he sheepishly said, 'That would be good.'

Ivan always took praying for the sick seriously, addressing specific ailments to the corresponding body parts. Having been delivered from a back problem himself, he has been particularly used in praying for those with such a condition.

In the confines of the police station, he prayed for the officer.

'I thank you for your prayer. Please, I don't want any trouble. I beg you to sign the paper and go back to your own country. If you don't, I fear for your life and for the lives of your friends. You are all in danger. If you insist on holding your healing mission those people who want to stop you will come and burn down the orphanage. If you don't sign it, I'll have to lock you up for your own safety.'

Ivan prayerfully considered his options. Stand firm and inflame an already explosive situation or submit. The safety of the children and those living at the orphanage lay heavily on his heart. They were his responsibility. He'd come to praise God and pray for the healing of the sick, not to endanger the lives of loved ones.

What do I do, Lord?

God-directed, he signed. With quick farewells they were soon on their way to Calcutta, praising God that no one had been hurt and everyone safe.

What appeared to be an end to the matter was just the beginning, as God's plan began to unfold. The group had no option but to remain in Calcutta for ten days until the return flight date.

The militants were extremely pleased at their triumph. Seizing their chance to publicise their success, they alerted a local correspondent. Had the report been confined to the state press, it would have been like so many neighbourhood incidents - a one-day wonder quickly forgotten. A greater power was at work - Creator God. The incident reached the national press.

Through this wide media cover, over 200 Indian Christian leaders contacted Solomon, each keen to support the work. Back home, it was suggested that a meeting be held with the pastors in India.

Not long after returning home, sad news reached Daphne. Her dad had developed a severe tummy upset. Despite intense hospital treatment, the illness did not abate. Solomon's friend and earthly protector slept in the Lord.

On hearing that Mr Soraine was dead, Matthew's relative renewed his aggression. He verbally threatened to harm Solomon, Sweta and the family.

A Listening Ear

The first Pastors' Conference in Bhubaneswar, the capital of Odisha, was successful. Sixty pastors from all around the area arrived to hear what God had laid on the hearts of Andrew, Ivan and Solomon. They taught Bible truths, held healing meetings and offered organisational advice and spiritual encouragement.

A second conference was held in Vizag, in Andhra Pradesh where over 150 pastors attended.

The orphanage was functioning well. Forty boys, a few helpers and a couple of widows who Solomon had taken off the streets for their protection worked harmoniously.

Solomon was deep in sleep when disturbing thoughts troubled him. Pictures of young illiterate girls, nothing more than slaves, ill-treated by their masters, beaten and starved, invaded his sleep.

Waking distressed, he wondered what help he could give. The orphanage was not big enough to take in girls. Trusting God, he prayed that He would direct.

Meanwhile the dispute over ownership of the orphanage was dragging on. The decision of the court was in Ivan's favour. Once settled, no more threats or demands for the building were possible. The deeds to the building and surrounding area were legally registered to 'The Spirit of Liberty Charity'.

Almost a year later, Solomon had another dream. In it, he was holding Ivan's hand and was led to a large building - a centre of learning with a place to worship. The pictures so real, on waking, he rang Ivan. He listened intently and said with much enthusiasm and abundant faith in a loving God, 'If it's God's will, He will pay the bill. I'll be with you soon. We'll talk then.'

With limited time in the country, Ivan's visit was intense. Travelling extensively, they preached and held further healing meetings. In some areas, the conditions were so harsh and disease rampant, they slept under the stars, abstaining from eating and surviving on bottled water.

After an exhaustive 12-hour journey over rough terrain followed by a further 3-hour walk to a remote area, they arrived at their destination. Met by a jubilant throng praising God for their safe arrival, personal desires melted away. A humbling occasion, the joyous people insisted on washing the visitors' feet. The love shown by those far less endowed with worldly wealth to the point of impoverishment, was beyond comprehension.

That day, many asked Jesus into their lives and were baptised, despite the infested village pool swarming with insects, frogs and snakes.

Ivan has witnessed many water baptisms in novel as well as more conventional settings. He would comfortably lead worship at the lakeside or riverbank in beautiful alpine settings. However, he readily admitted he preferred the locals taking to the Indian waters!

Following much prayer over Solomon's dream, they took a step in faith and decided to plan for a much larger orphanage, accommodating both boys and young girls, and big enough to house a learning centre with a place to worship. As to where the money for such an establishment would come from, was a matter of faith. The visit a success, it was time to return home.

Four weeks later, back in Britain, Ivan's joy continued as Solomon wrote to say that many were still accepting

Jesus as their Saviour. Some who'd not heard the gospel at that time had arrived at various pastors' houses saying they wanted the same God who had healed their relatives.

After further prayer, Ivan directed Solomon to purchase land large enough to accommodate 100 children and a Bible School for prospective pastors.

August 2008 was a particularly difficult time for Christians in Odisha. Maoists, [Indian communists] allegedly murdered a prominent anti-Christian Hindu. This murder sparked off a rebellion against Christians. Militant Hindus rampaged through the villages, murdering innocent Christians. Over 500 men, women and children were killed. Hundreds of churches were destroyed and over 52 000 people were displaced - many hid in the forests. Christians were threatened to re-convert to Hinduism. Those who refused, fled their homes or faced death. Solomon, Sweta and the children at the orphanage were not immune from such trauma.

Threats and Violence

A relative of Matthew - a renowned street fighter - made claim to the building. With the full weight of the law behind him, he pursued his ownership through the courts. An unforeseen problem had arisen when setting up the orphanage resulting in a costly and time-consuming period for Ivan. An unsettling period for the residents, the threat of eviction was never far away.

'I need £3000!' demanded the man.

'I haven't 3000 rupees - never mind £3000!' said Solomon.

'Then get it quickly. If you don't, I'll kill you and the kids.'

The street fighter's demand was not just words aimed to alarm, scare or terrify a loved one. Physical violence would follow if not given the cash.

Meanwhile, the man commenced court proceedings to acquire the building. The threats continued.

Ivan, fearing for Solomon and the children's lives. He had no money to send. In faith, he said, 'Tell the man he can have his money, and that I want the deeds of the property transferred to the Spirit of Liberty Charity.'

With heavy heart, he replaced the receiver and prayed. 'I can't do anything, Lord. Sort it out.'

Again he held to the promise of Jesus.

"Ask and it shall be given you, Seek and you shall find. Knock and it shall be opened onto you," (Matthew 7:7).

After a preaching engagement a woman approached him.

'I have to give you some money for God's work in India. Let me have your address and I'll send you a cheque.'

'Do you want me to use it for the children or to buy something for the orphanage?'

'Use it for whatever you think fit.'

Ten days later, he cashed a cheque for £3 000. God had provided the exact amount to pay off the man - not a penny more.

The rays of the sun beamed heat and light over the village, awakening the residents to an uneasy 'presence'. The early morning bustle of activity was absent. Strangers had arrived.

Sweta was preparing breakfast when raised voices intensified into angry shouting. Solomon rushed to the window. A group of men wielding sticks had gathered in the street. Sweta screamed when the door burst open.

'You'd best flee to the forest, Solomon,' said a friend. 'There's an angry mob gathering. They're after you. They're threatening to burn the orphanage.'

'I must go and see what is happening,' he insisted.

'If you go there, the mob will kill you!' said the concerned friend.

'I must! The children will be terrified.'

'I've sent the children to school. There's only a couple of helpers still there. It's you the mob's after. There's no time. You must hide. I'll see to things at the orphanage.'

'Go, Solomon!' urged Sweta. 'I'll stay here. They'll not attack me.' Such was her faith, she knew that Jesus was watching over her and the children.

Hesitant to leave her, he prayed for God's protection and then slipped quietly into the forest.

Stirred up by agitators spreading resentment and hate, the mob grew in number. The shouting and jeering intensified and many brandished sticks. Some had knives, inciting others to attack unprotected children and adults in revenge for actions allegedly undertaken at some distant place of which many of the riotous people had never even heard.

It would take a miracle if the orphanage was to survive. Angry men approached the foundations to the new building, ready to destroy the work. As brave villagers entered the streets to confront the aggressors, tense moments followed. Angry voices and turbulence gave way to the firm voice of reason.

Gradually, the antagonistic mob stopped their actions as moderate men persuaded many to go home. Soon, the calming influence subdued the rage.

There was much rejoicing when Solomon returned home. Yet again, a time to thank Jesus for keeping everyone safe.

Reports were circulating that as a result of the violence, 60 000 Christians had taken refuge in forests as fundamentalists brandishing weapons attacked them.

The whole area of Odisha was troubled as finger-pointing, violence, rape and murder on a large scale spread its contaminated tentacles across the state. Many misguided, ill-informed people were engaged in a doctrine of hate towards minority sections of the populous.

Within the week, at least 26 people had been killed by extremist violence in Odisha and 4 000 Christian homes were destroyed, along with several churches and convents. There were wrongs done to Christians, Muslims and Hindus alike, as the rampant violence spiralled out of control.

Overwhelming Compassion

On hearing of the widows' and orphans' dire straits, Solomon, along with a number of pastors, travelled hundreds of miles to see for themselves.

Nothing had prepared them for the utter misery, denigration and destitution as they walked deeper into the forest. Small camps of frightened people clinging to fragmented hope were scattered throughout the heavily wooded area. Denied food and shelter, they depended on the flora for shade and fruit from the trees to sustain them.

Personal hygiene was not high on the list of priorities as psychological trauma at seeing loved ones burned in their own homes, or brutally raped and murdered by unloving people taunted them. Reduced to living rough, homeless and abandoned by society, prayer was all they had. Sadly, such suffering was too much for some who longed for Jesus to take them.

In such hopelessness, Solomon felt indolent. He wept. God had brought him far from home to experience the depths to which humans can sink. Yet, a faint glimmer of hope flickered in the darkness. He was witnessing the result of ignorance, intolerance and evil wrought by hardened fanatics on those who loved Jesus.

The true meaning of persecution was evident wherever he trod. He longed to make things right by transporting everyone to the orphanage for sanctuary. This could not be. There were thousands of men, women and children of all ages hiding in the forest. Solomon and the other pastors did what they could to bring relief.

His heart overstretched reality as he agreed to return home with 10 widows and 15 children.

Accommodating so many in the orphanage proved difficult with limited toilet facilities. Illness and disease was a real concern. Six months later, the overcrowding was so acute, a number of widows returned to the forest.

Through this heart-rending time of Christian persecution, Ivan and Solomon worked hard to ensure a new orphanage would be built.

On one of Ivan's visits, it took Solomon and a small group of pastors an eleven-hour journey by jeep through a forest plagued with monkeys, buffalos and rats to meet with the destitute believers. Seven hours into the journey, the route became impassable. Leaving the driver and jeep, they walked a number of hours in heat of 40 degrees.

On reaching the settlement, the party was overwhelmed by the welcome. Everyone rushed to greet them with singing, dancing, shaking of tambourines and maracas. Ivan felt deeply moved by what was happening. Full of joy, the people embraced him as a matter of respect and washed the visitors' feet.

He was grateful for the rest when seated beneath a tree enjoying the shade. Later that day, over 150 passionate Christians listened with great interest as first one speaker and then another shared God's Word.

Driven from their homes and fearful to return for fear of being murdered, the forest dwellers showed their love for Jesus as they worshipped and prayed for deliverance. There in the midst of adversity, strife and insecurity, each believer was filled with God's Spirit. Ivan prayed for the sick and many were healed.

Time only allowed a short stay as the walk back would be difficult. Each felt privileged to have witnessed such enduring love and thanked God for taking them there.

Four hours into the walk, they were thankful to see the smiling driver, ready to take them to their hotel, where they could enjoy hot baths, air conditioned rooms and a good night's sleep.

The considerate love of Jesus had caused the driver to wait for over 40 hours in the stifling heat of the day and crippling cold nights with only water to sustain him. Truly a labour of love.

On another occasion, the party undertook a four-hour journey by car through the jungle. They'd travelled in the heat of the day for two hours when a lorry loaded high with iron bars couldn't climb a hill. It slid back and blocked the road. Ivan was undeterred.

'Chop down a few trees to widen the road.'

This they did and after two and a half hours, the police re-opened the highway. With only a further 8 miles to travel, again the way became impassable, with walking the only option. A few hours later, singing filled their ears as the villagers came out to greet them. The teaching of God's Word, worship and prayer for the sick followed. A windstorm was threatening. Locals advised the visitors to leave before the way back became too muddy to pass. Returning hours later, they arrived safely at their hotel.

There was time to relax next day as Solomon and Ivan took the children to the beach. They played games, enjoyed ice creams and the fresh evening breeze before returning to the orphanage. The following day, Ivan preached on 'Seek you first the kingdom of God'. Six souls gave their hearts to Jesus.

The next night he held a healing service at which the waiter from the hotel asked Jesus into his life. Many were healed. Returning to Britain, Ivan spoke to India through livestream media.

A further conference was planned. Taking a step in faith, Ivan promised to supply a bicycle to each pastor present.

Thinking not many would attend, he was pleasantly surprised when almost double the number expected, arrived.

How would he raise £5 000 for 100 bikes?

Those back home became his answer to prayer.

Thankful for a Bathtub

Ivan was at home when the phone rang.

'It's me, Ivan! Enzo.'

Ivan was delighted. His brother lived 200 miles away.

'How are you, Enzo?'

'That's what I'm ringing you about. I'm in hospital.'

Ivan was stunned and saddened. Confident that Jesus could heal him, he asked, 'Have you prayed about it?'

A minor hesitation brought the firm answer, 'No.'

'You ought to. If you ask Jesus into your life, I'm sure He'll heal you.'

'I wish I could be certain.'

'You can be. Certainty is about trusting Jesus by engaging faith. We all live in the present, but of this I am certain - the future is in God's hands. God cares for me eternally. I know you believe in God.'

'I do.'

'Well, it's like this. God sent his son Jesus into this world to stand in our place so that we can have direct access and fellowship with Him. Jesus, being innocent and above reproach, became the ultimate sacrifice by dying for us. He was laughed at, scourged with a whip, beaten and nailed to a cross. He died a most gruesome death. That was not the end. Having died, He rose on the third day and ascended into heaven where He sits beside God the Father. You can read all about Him in the Bible.

'One day He's coming back for us to be with Him forever. I'm getting excited!'

'It's all right for you. You know Him.'

'So can you! Everyone can have a personal relationship with Him. Jesus died so we can live with

Him and have abundant life - not in material things or monetary value, but in spiritual riches.

'It took me 42 years to even think about Him. You know how I lived. I was godless. I knew nothing of the love of Jesus until He showed me the way to life. Knowing Jesus is not about believing in something that is dead, redundant or carved out of wood, moulded in clay or chipped out of marble. Neither is knowing Jesus about bowing down to any man-made imagery or praying to the air in the hope that someone is out there listening. Those who invite Jesus into their lives soon discover that He is alive and wants to be their Friend.

'Don't take my word for it. I'm not going to persuade you either way. You saw the change He made in my life. I wish I could give you what I experience and how I feel towards Jesus. I can't. You have to want to know Him yourself. Then and only then, will you know and understand what I've been telling you these last years. God really does love you, Enzo. But, I add, there can be no salvation without first asking Jesus to forgive you your sin.'

Enzo listened intently.

There was a long pause. Ivan thought he'd said too much. He'd not intended to preach to him. This was no pre-planned speech or hastily concocted talk. He said what God had laid on his heart spontaneously and without pre-conceived thoughts.

'I don't know how to ask Jesus into my life.'

'Do you want to know Him?'

'I do.'

'May I pray with you?'

'I'd like that.'

'Are you sure? I don't want to force you into saying anything you don't mean.'

'I'm sure.'

'Would you like to repeat what I say? Please, don't say a word if you don't really mean it or decide you don't want to meet with Jesus.'

Ivan was conscious of his brother's vulnerability. Neither did Ivan want to talk his brother into agreeing to things he might regret later. Torn between wanting his brother to meet Jesus as he himself had done, and fearful of pressurising him, he again asked, 'Are you sure you want to meet Jesus?'

'I'm sure, Ivan. I'm sure.'

Still he questioned himself. *I've never hesitated when others wanted to meet with Jesus. Why should I now?* 'Repeat these words after me. Dear Jesus, I know that I am a sinner and seek your forgiveness.'

Enzo repeated each word.

'I really want to know you. I invite you into my life. Please forgive me of all the wrong I have done in the past.'

Enzo repeated Ivan's prayer.

'You need to pause for a moment and think about all the wrong things you've done in your life. Don't tell me. You need to tell Jesus. Your past is between Jesus and you. I'm here to guide you through your prayer. It's by God's gift of love and His grace that we come to know Jesus.'

Enzo thought, and then said, 'You can continue now.'

Ivan pressed the phone tightly against his ear. 'Dear Jesus, I ask that you become my Friend and Saviour.'

Enzo was tearful as he repeated the words, knowing that Jesus loved him.

'Start praying and reading your Bible every day,' advised Ivan lovingly. 'Look for a church you can go to.' A few private words followed and then Ivan asked, 'Do you believe that Jesus can heal you?'

'I do.'

Ivan prayed for his brother's healing, and then they talked about Jesus' love before saying a fond farewell.

A few days later, Enzo rang.

'I'm home, Ivan!' he said excitedly. 'I'm healed!'

The following day, Enzo drove the 200 miles north to knock on Ivan's door.

'I've come to be baptised,' he blurted out before Ivan could welcome him in. 'Where can I be baptised?'

'You'd best come in.'

Soon a hot cup of coffee was in Enzo's hands.

'You can baptise me at your church. We can go now.'

'Hang on a minute, Enzo. It takes gallons of water to baptise you and I need to set up the baptistery. It's only an inflatable pool!'

'How about the sea?'

Ivan laughed as he pictured standing with his brother in freezing water in the middle of winter.

'I've a better idea. I'll baptise you in the bathtub.'

'Fine by me!'

Phailin

Solomon's urgent text to Ivan was infused with despair.

'A cyclone is to hit Deeipur within the hour. It's estimated to have wind speeds of 142-149 mph bringing with it a storm surge of up to 19 feet. Pray for us all. Pray for us, Papa! Pray for us!'

Suddenly everything went dead. No telephone, no text, Ivan felt helpless. The only source of news would be radio and television.

Two hours later at around 9.30 p.m., Cyclone Phailin made landfall, slamming into Gopalpur on the east coast of Odisha at over 120 mph, bringing a storm surge of 10 to 12 feet where the sea rose up pushing water miles inland. With a width of 1000 miles, Deeipur lay in the direct path of Phailin.

Ivan could only imagine what was happening to his extended family on that October Saturday.

Those of the fellowship throughout Europe prayed intently that God would protect the children and families who were suffering a nightmare of gigantic proportion. The last time a cyclone had hit Odisha in 1999 it had killed more than 10 000 people.

Not only had the intense storm cloud over India covered the land, it had penetrated the hearts of every believer who prayed. The natural attribute of concern, instilled by God as a part of His love, was well exercised by His people. Hope, trust and faith were truly tested as no news intensified anxiety, generating focussed prayer. Daily, every church in the fellowship contacted Ivan. It was hard for him to say, 'No news.'

Trusting Jesus that He would take care of those loved ones in India, the Apostle Paul's words became an increasing source of encouragement.

And we know that in all things God works for the good of those who love him, who have been called according to his purpose (Romans 8:28).

With all communication blocked, long agonising hours of waiting for news stretched out to days, as each minute seemed an hour and each day a year. All anyone could do was pray for God's blessing and protection for all those gripped in the turmoil and destruction.

Emotions were running high as every email and phone call brought the inevitable stomach-churning. Six nail-biting days passed without news. Then the phone call that had been so long in coming reached Ivan.

'Thank you for praying for us, Papa. We're alive!'

Inexplicable joy washed over him when hearing Solomon's first words.

The news was not all good. It could, however, have been far worse without constant prayer.

Solomon gave an appraisal of the situation in Deeipur.

'The children are safe, but are in hospital. Some are very ill. None are injured. We endured and survived the cyclone. Wind, rain and flood overtook us. Everything was soaked. Our mattresses, sheets and clothes are all ruined. We have nowhere to sleep. We moved all the children into a small room for safety. We've no means of cooking or drying ourselves out. The deluge destroyed our generator. We're surviving on rice. The cyclone brought down power and communication lines. Locals say it could take one to three months to restore. We struggled on for days, and then our water became polluted. The children caught tummy upsets. We had to take them to Baranpour Hospital 12 miles away. We have an infestation of river snakes that are troublesome, but that's the least of our concerns. The flood is slowly subsiding. Everywhere is damp and smelly.'

'Buy what you need, Solomon - clothes, mattresses, bedding. I'll leave it up to you to decide. I know God will provide the money. Get the electrics checked and then have a new generator installed.'

'There's a large crack in the main wall of the orphanage and we have roofing problems.'

'Have it fixed, Solomon.'

The storm had been the worst they'd known. Illness had intensified their trauma.

The devastation to the rest of the village was horrific. The cyclone had blown away many houses. Buildings were destroyed, horticultural fields flooded, trees uprooted and roads were blocked. The cyclone had affected 1 300 families living in the village, leaving many homeless, wet, cold and hungry. Despair reigned until a light shone as those who'd opposed Jesus Christ approached Solomon.

'Help us. We have no food, no houses,' they pleaded.

Compassion overwhelmed him. Knowing God was with him, he told Ivan, who, lovingly offered hope in the middle of chaos.

'Make sure each villager receives 25 kilo of rice, a blanket, a torch, a drum of oil, yellow lentils and dhal.' Amazingly, a five-figure amount was raised and sent to Solomon, who bought and distributed the provisions.

To have minimal damage and everyone safe was a miracle.

Great news followed when believers invited Solomon to present the gospel to over 1000 people in Andhra Pradesh. An invitation he did not refuse!

Epilogue

Ivan's enthusiasm to tell people of Jesus' love continues to grow. Recently called to the Balkans, God has opened a door to meet with pastors of various churches, sharing with them the Apostle Paul's teaching as outlined in his letter to the Ephesians.

This *'compassionate father, with the zeal of a youth'* continues to present the gospel in both word and action and never tires in carrying 'the fragrance of Jesus' wherever he goes.

On meeting Jesus, Ivan found that His love is the reason to live, and longs for others to experience that love.

For those who want to invite Jesus into their life and are unsure how to speak with Him, Ivan offers his guidance on the next page.

Your Invitation

Knowing Jesus is about enjoying a personal relationship with Him. God sent His one and only Son into this world because He loves each one of us. Jesus died to enable you and me to have union with God. The wonderful thing is that God raised Jesus from the dead! He is alive!

If you really want to know Jesus, think for a moment and then say these words aloud.

Dear Jesus, I know that I am a sinner and ask for forgiveness. I really want to know you. I invite you into my life.

Pause for a moment and think about all the wrong things you have done in your life, then say,

Dear Jesus, I ask that you become my friend and Saviour, Amen.

What next?
Tell someone. Your spoken words often reaffirm your actions.

Start to read the Bible.
It's good to read a little each day. The Gospel of Mark is a good place to start. Study each verse and ask Jesus to help you understand the meaning.

Speak to Jesus often.
Don't be afraid to tell Him your smallest concerns. Trust Him and ask for His guidance. He's your best Friend and loves hearing from you.

Share fellowship with other believers.

Jesus wants you to have fellowship with others who love Him. Find a church where you feel comfortable and that adheres to God's Word, the Bible. Ask Jesus to show you at which church He wants you to worship.

Note

You will have read in this book about God's gift - His Holy Spirit. God's Spirit led you to Jesus. His Spirit will help you to become strong in faith and love. Prayer is the key, trust the action and joy in knowing Jesus is the result of placing your faith in a Creator God who loves you.

Words of encouragement.

How great is the love the Father has lavished on us, that we should be called children of God! And that is what we are! The reason the world does not know us is that it did not know him. Dear friends, now we are children of God, and what we will be has not yet been made known. But we know that when Christ appears, we shall be like him, for we shall see him as he is. All who have this hope in him purify themselves, just as he is pure (1 John 3:1-3).

Blessings

Ivan

Author's Notes

How I came to write 'Love a Reason to Live' is truly amazing. Little did I know that divine appointments would govern each event.

A range of perfectly-timed scenarios mark its conception since being told of Ivan by Angelo whose biography 'Change Me' I had the privilege of writing.

My initial contact with Ivan was a short email telling him we must meet. Pressing the *send* key, I felt I should have explained more fully. Too late! My email was somewhere in cyber space.

A week passed and then a reply. Apprehensive as to the response, I prayed that the first line would be positive.

Dear Sam, I'd love to meet with you, were Ivan's words.

Unbeknown to me, God's plan was already in motion.

Two years passed and we had still not met. Our meeting was advanced when my daughter and her husband who had unexpectedly moved to Glasgow, turned up at the church at which Ivan attended.

A year later, everything pointed to Jesus bringing us together. We sat in his office in a church building in central Glasgow.

My job was to acquire his agreement to include him in the book, 'Change Me!', interview him, and then depart. There I was, scribbling for all my worth, trying desperately not to miss any salient points, when halfway through the interview, his mobile phone rang. With a big smile covering his face, he turned his phone towards me. It was the boys in Odisha, India, singing in English,

'Happy Birthday to you!' I felt privileged to share in his joy and sensed genuine love in their voices for the man they called 'Papa'. Here was no ordinary man, but one touched by God. The brief phone call at an end, I had a tear in my eye as I again took up my pencil to question and write.

My job was done. Stashing my notes away, I prepared to leave.

'I tried writing my story,' said Ivan sadly. 'I wrote a couple of pages and realised it was too much for me to do.'

I said nothing.

'I speak the language, but writing is so different. In my desperation, I screwed up the papers and threw them in the bin. *I can't write it!* I cried out to Jesus. *Send me someone to write it for me.* I was so distraught I opened my email and there was your letter.'

Ivan believed God had sent me to write his story. Everything seemed right and was pointing to the fact that I should write about him.

The confirmation which God gave is contained within these pages.

In closing, no earthly individual can take credit for guiding, providing and sustaining such undertakings as described in this book. The glory rightly belongs to God.

Recent publication by the same author

ISBN 9780955766466

A story of stubborn resistance to God's call, it questions the acceptance of coincidence as an excuse to deny the existence of a loving God and sacrificial Saviour, Jesus Christ.

Centred on hardened spiritual outlaws intent on destroying themselves, this remarkable true story reveals how God lifted them out of spiritual darkness by showing them Jesus.

It highlights how God, equipped and harnessed the abilities of several strangers from four continents - long before they met - to play a small part in the telling of God's Glory and the love He has for us through His gift of grace.

Also available on Amazon Kindle.

Please consider donating to the ongoing work of the Spirit of Liberty Orphanage.

Destiny Ministries (Indian Orphanage), 1120 Pollokshaws Road, Glasgow, G41 3QP.

Please accept my one off gift of £10☐ £20☐ £50☐ £☐

Please make cheques payable to **Destiny Ministries (Indian Orphanage Account).**

To give by monthly standing order

Please pay to: The Royal Bank of Scotland

Glasgow City Branch (A)

10 Gordon Street

Glasgow

G1 3PL

Sort code 83-44-00 For the credit of Destiny Ministries' Account Number 00230620

The sum of £☐ until further notice.

Date of first payment to be ☐☐☐☐☐☐

Your Account Details

Name of Bank or Building Society ☐

Address of Bank or Building Society ☐

Account Holder's Name ☐

Account Number ☐☐☐☐☐☐☐☐ Sort Code ☐☐☐☐☐☐

Your Details

Name ☐

Address ☐

Post Code

Signature ☐

Gift Aid ☐ I wish all the donations made to **Destiny Ministries** since **6th April 2008** and all donations made thereafter to be treated as Gift Aid Donations.

Notes

Notes

Notes

Notes

Notes

Notes

Notes

Notes

Notes

Notes

Notes

Notes

Notes

Notes